T0301199

The Path We Run

The Path We Run

A Personal History of
Women's Ultrarunning

Jen Benson

First published in Great Britain in 2024 by Cassell, an imprint of
Octopus Publishing Group Ltd
Carmelite House
50 Victoria Embankment
London EC4Y 0DZ
www.octopusbooks.co.uk

An Hachette UK Company
www.hachette.co.uk

ISBN 978-1-78840-437-2

A CIP catalogue record for this book is available from the British Library.

Typeset in 11.5/17pt Sabon LT Pro by Jouve (UK), Milton Keynes

Printed and bound in Great Britain.

1 3 5 7 9 10 8 6 4 2

This FSC® label means that materials used
for the product have been responsibly sourced.

To the ultrarunners – past, present and future

CONTENTS

INTRODUCTION

It's December. Cool air slides off the surface of Ullswater, meeting my cheek with a hint of winter's bite. As the light dims, the bulky fells that rise to my right darken; details fade, paths become indistinct.

I've been running all day. Hours melting into hours. The tick, tick, tick of my feet on the trail marking the passing of something that is both time and distance and yet, in the usual way, neither of these things. On a really long run, measures of space and time take on an altered meaning. Perspective shifts.

People sometimes ask me why I run. But I've been doing it for so long now, my entire self – and sense of self – shaped by the forces of running, that I have no idea who I am without it. I'd need a good reason not to run.

Running is the ultimate freedom to fidget. The antidote to restlessness. Walking's good, but not as good as running. That rhythmical movement, just violent enough to shake you out of apathy at each step. A metronomic reminder: *Here I am here I am here I am. . .*

When I'm walking, my mind wanders with my feet. Rebecca Solnit wrote that the mind, like the feet at walking pace, works at about three miles an hour – 'the speed of thought, or thoughtfulness'.

But running hauls you out of reverie. It's more focused than walking and brings more clarity to the mind. Faster running brings sudden realizations; with long, slow runs, it's more a kind of fertile emergence. I have my most productive thoughts when I'm out on a run that's moderate in both pace and distance. Not too much effort, but just enough. Ideal growing conditions. The post-run shower is a good place for thinking, too.

Today, I've been running the Ullswater Way from Pooley Bridge. An anticlockwise loop around the Cumbrian lake that has given me so much more than simply running. Adventure is probably an overused word, but I think it's a good description of a long run in a beautiful place. As I watch the village I set out from this morning gradually draw close again, lights glowing a welcome into the dusk, it feels like a triumphal return. I honestly feel like I've been on an adventure.

The route is about 32 kilometres (20 miles) long, but I made some detours. I explored the summit of Gowbarrow Fell, where the wind hit me with a force that whipped my words away as I tried to have a conversation with a couple I met at the trig point. I stopped to stare at Aira Force, awestruck by the power of the waterfall as I experienced it from both above, looking down, and below, looking up.

A little further on, I met a friend who'd parked her car and run out to meet me. We shared a few miles, enjoying both company and the peace of the place, rounding the lake's southwestern extremity, passing Patterdale, Side Farm, Silver Bay. Then she returned to her car and I continued solo, more aware of my aloneness than I'd been before.

A little later still, I shared the length of a field with another woman, who was running the Tour de Helvellyn, a 61-kilometre (38-mile) winter mountain ultra. We chatted and I asked her about the race; she said she'd missed a lot of training and it wasn't going as well as she'd hoped. Soon, she powered ahead, looking strong and comfortable despite the missed training – and despite having run twice as far and over a lot more hills than I had.

Now, in the final mile or so of my run, I have that sense of satisfaction of a challenge successfully completed. I chose this route; no one else suggested it or helped me plan it. I didn't get lost – or at least not problematically so. I attended to my food and water needs; I enjoyed a few miles with company and more alone. I navigated my internal world as well as circumnavigating the lake, managing my emotions, interpreting my body's signs and signals, breathing through moments of anxiety, revelling in moments of joy.

There's something else I've noticed as I've run today: the footprints in the mud beneath my feet. I can pick out those belonging to trail and fell shoes – distinctly different from those made by walking boots – and in places like this there are a lot of them. Running on trails forges a sense of connection with those who have run before me – I'm literally running in their footsteps. I wonder how their adventures were, how they experienced time, distance, company or aloneness. What they saw and felt along the way. I think of the women – women like me and those I've run with today, who, not so long ago, would never have been afforded the freedom to have an adventure like this one. And those who went out and did it anyway – in the dark, in disguise, with male allies – creating a new path for women to run.

IN THE FOOTSTEPS
OF LEGENDS

'Whenever you find yourself doubting how far
you can go, just remember how far you have come.
Remember everything you have faced, all the battles
you have won, and all the fears you have overcome.
Then raise your head high and forge ahead knowing
you've got this!'

—Jacky Hunt-Broersma, cancer survivor,
amputee, world record holder for
running 104 marathons in
104 consecutive days

'm in my early 40s when I realize I'm not who I used
to be. It's nothing dramatic. Just a gradual process of
change; subtle and drawn-out to the point of being barely
noticeable. A gradual evolution over years of thinking I was
just being myself, followed by the abrupt realization that I
might actually be someone completely different. Not that
long ago, I was someone who did hard, scary things for fun.
I'd jump at chances to go on almost any adventure, with

almost anyone who asked. Now though, the thought of doing almost anything with an elevated level of objective risk has me running for home.

At home – the comfortable, cozy space I share with Sim, our children and our dog – there's an old photo. Taken at the finish of a mountain marathon years ago, it's of younger versions of Sim and me, smiling into the camera, arms casually slung over each other's shoulders. We look tired in a relaxed kind of way; carefree, untethered. We also look a bit smug, having just finished two days of self-navigated, self-supported running over rough, pathless terrain and done pretty well.

I'm so used to this photo that most days I barely see it. But today, for some reason, it catches my eye. I stop to look at it – really look at it – for the first time in years.

Sim looks young – ridiculously so. Fifteen years later, not that much has changed. We'd been together only a short time when the picture was taken, but it's clear I'm smitten. The first thing I'd noticed about Sim when I met him was his energy – he buzzes with it. He gets on with things, finishing them while everyone else is still wondering whether there's time to begin.

Glancing at the image of myself, I hardly recognize it. I look happy, but there's something else there, too. Fresh out of a failed marriage, exhilarated by the sense of possibility I'd found, I'd been braver, crazier, willing to give anything a go. Anything that didn't involve too much in the way of feelings, at least. Feeling left you open to hurt, embarrassment, dependence and shame. Back then, I'd been good with pain of the physical kind, but emotions didn't get a look in.

I'm struck by the gulf of time and life between then and now. Am I even the same person? In the story I tell myself, I'm still someone who relishes challenges, pushes limits, faces difficulties head-on. But is that really true? Rewritten and retextured by life and love, age and motherhood, perhaps not.

The photo conjures up memories of long days with only myself to think about, pushing my body hard, ignoring pain and fatigue, taking risks, managing not to die and drinking too much to celebrate.

I do none of those things now. Now, I help others devise grand adventures, and make sure those I have myself are fully risk-assessed and family-friendly. These days I don't even drink. I love being a mum and I'd willingly thrown myself into it, stepping away from doing anything too risky, too tiring, too lengthy. I've needed – and wanted – to be there for my children, to have energy to play with them, to read bedtime stories and comfort them when they woke in the night. We haven't spent a night apart since my daughter, Eva, was born, more than 12 years ago.

But now they're older, and need me differently, being a mother is no longer a reason – or an excuse – to avoid doing hard things. Instead, there's something else stopping me. These days, I worry about everything: work deadlines, whether my son's mild fever might actually be meningitis, social media, car crashes, the climate crisis, war. I don't think it's that I'm a pessimist or overly catastrophizing – these are all real, relevant issues in our modern world. It's that I'm happy feeling safe, happy with predictability and routine, happy with only doing the things I'm comfortable doing. Sometimes, if I don't leave the house for a whole day, I wonder whether I might never leave the house again. And yet, somewhere deep within, is a growing realization that there's another kind of life – one that's exciting, exhilarating, adventurous – and it's passing me by.

Coming out of the other side of mothering young children feels a little like stumbling out of the depths of a vast forest, blinking in a new bright light of possibility. In some ways, I know my former self is there, waiting for me. But in others, the experiences I've been through have shaped me into someone entirely different. I'm softer, slower now, more contemplative and more afraid. I've opened myself up to feelings and emotions and love. This is, in almost every way, a life that makes me deeply happy. But I can't quiet the voice asking whether I've still got it in me to do big, hard, scary things. I still yearn for that elusive feeling of pushing myself to my mental and physical limits, keeping going when I don't know how and looking back on it all with a deep sense of satisfaction.

I'm intrigued to know whether I can still do the things the old me – the one in the photo – did. Whether, having shed the fearless resilience of youth, the perspective, wisdom and endurance gained through being a nearly middle-aged mother are enough.

* * *

Ever since the first time I ran further than a marathon, back in the hazy past of my 20s, I've been fascinated by the idea of running 100 miles. Even when the kids were tiny, and doing it was something I had neither the time nor energy for, I was entranced by the 100-mile distance and those who ran it. Over the years, the books and articles I've read, the films I've watched and the stories I've listened to have fed this fire. The names of the famous 100-milers hold a magic and allure that I can't escape: the Western States Endurance Run, the Hardrock 100, the Ultra-Trail du Mont Blanc (UTMB). I've pored over the scientific literature on our bodies and brains under the stresses of ultramarathons and read countless books about other people's adventures over 100 miles and longer, battling through nausea and sleep deprivation, fatigued and footsore on the trails, finishing forever changed by their experiences.

Covering 100 miles (161 kilometres) on foot strikes that ideal balance of improbable yet possible. It's an intriguing puzzle: running through an entire night, the kit, the fuelling, the self-management, the psychological skills. Some 100-milers involve mountains or other rough terrain, navigation, or winter conditions. As 14-times Western States champion Ann Trason once said, 'I've always just looked at 100 miles as life in a day. You have all the trials and tribulations of a life in one day.'

Nonetheless, running such a long way – including running through a whole night and perhaps even two – hasn't ever been something I've felt ready to do myself. When the kids were little, sleep was often so scarce that the idea of voluntarily giving up a night in my bed seemed like folly. Now, though, as they inch towards their teenage years and the challenge has become waking them up, I begin to wonder if it's time to give it a go.

The seed of the idea lodges and won't go away. I follow other people's journeys to conquering the 100-mile distance – the training, the research, the Big Day, the finish-line celebrations and post-race retellings – and imagine myself going through the same. I see women, including mums, in their 40s, 50s and beyond achieving incredible feats of endurance and realize I desperately want to feel that too. Then, in the summer of 2021, British doctor Beth Pascall wins Western States, finishing in the second-fastest time by a woman (only Ellie Greenwood, another British runner, had gone faster) and seventh overall. Second- and third-placed women, Ruth Croft and Ragna Debats, also finish in the top 10 overall, while half of the top 30 finishers are women. It's a phenomenal day for women's ultrarunning and I'm utterly captivated.

I decide, there and then, that I'm going to train for and run a 100-mile race. The idea terrifies me but, in many ways, that's part of the appeal. Right now, when it comes to doing hard things, I don't know who I am any more. But I do know that throwing myself at this goal of running 100 miles will help me work it out. I also know that, if I'm successful, I'll have some pretty strong evidence that the part of me that once relished discomfort and tough physical challenges is still there.

* * *

Women's access to sport, and to muddy, sweaty, outdoors sport in particular, has been a contentious issue throughout history. Women weren't permitted in the gymnasia of the ancient world, and only the Spartans actively encouraged women to exercise – for the purposes of bearing strong male warriors.

Yet still there are stories of strong, powerful, athletic women in ancient history, from Cleopatra and Boudicca to Eva's favourite (to my delight), the Greek princess Atalanta of Boeotia.

Atalanta's father, King Schoeneus, had longed for a son and heir and, in his disappointment at the birth of a daughter, left the infant girl to die on Mount Parthenion. But Atalanta was discovered by a she-bear whose cubs had been recently killed by hunters. The bear nursed the child until she was eventually discovered by the hunters who raised her themselves in the mountains.

At home in the wilderness, Atalanta grew up to be a skilled archer and phenomenal runner, avoiding men and slaying two randy centaurs. On returning to her father's house, she was at last accepted by the king, who promptly decided to marry her off. Atalanta agreed, but (knowing she was a faster runner than any man) only on the condition that any future husband must first beat her in a foot race. Eventually, she was tricked into marrying a minor mythological figure, Hippomenes, in a cunning scheme devised by the goddess Aphrodite. But it's the story of Atlanta's fearlessness and athleticism that's endured, and that's captured my daughter's imagination.

Women's track and field events were not included in the Olympic Games until Amsterdam in 1928, when three running events were held: the 100 metre, 4 x 100-metre relay and 800 metre. But it was the 800-metre race that would be remembered, and not with good reason. Nine women lined up at the start and all of them finished, with six breaking the previous world record. Lina Radke of Germany won the gold medal in 2:16:8, taking 7 seconds off the previous world record.

Despite its apparent success, however, the race was not well received by the global press. In fact, the sight of a group of athletic women running powerfully around the track – bare, muscular limbs pumping; bodies sweating; faces gurning – seemed to be both shocking and unacceptable.

In the UK, *The Times* called the race 'dangerous', while the *London Daily Mail* suggested it was too difficult for women. The US and Canadian press echoed these sentiments, with the *Chicago Tribune* reporting that five women collapsed after the race, and that fifth-place finisher Florence MacDonald needed to be 'worked over' after 'falling onto the grass unconscious'. The *Montreal Daily Star* called the race a 'disgrace', suggesting that running 800 metres was 'obviously beyond women's powers of endurance, and can only be injurious to them'. One reporter incorrectly claimed that only six women finished the race and that five of them collapsed, concluding: 'It was not a very edifying spectacle to see a group of fine girls running themselves into a state of exhaustion.'

The devastating result was the immediate withdrawal of women's running from the Olympic Games and it would not return until 1960. But why did the 1928 800-metre race cause such a stir?

Governing bodies at the time cited 'scientific evidence' as the reason why women's running events should not be a part of the Olympics. Historians Patricia Vertinksy and Martha Verbrugge highlight the dominant narrative of the late 19th and early 20th centuries, in which women were seen as frail and physically incapable, limiting what was acceptable in a sporting context. Exertion, and its toll on the energy reserves of a woman, particularly during menstruation, was not encouraged.

Long-distance swimming, being a less obviously vigorous (though no less demanding) sport that, unlike running, kept the sporting female body well hidden, was considered more acceptable. In 1926, Gertrude Ederle became the first woman to swim the English Channel – beating the men's record in the process – and was praised by the media. Interestingly, the press had no concerns about her levels of exhaustion or energy deficit after more than 14 hours in the water. Instead, it was noted how fresh she appeared after completing the task.

Delving further into the 100-year-old 'science' behind the recommendation that women shouldn't run, I find that menstruation and its draining effects on women's energy reserves and ability to exercise are often blamed. This represents an interesting parallel with an emerging field of sport science today, where interest in the menstrual cycle and its potential to impact on the female body's ability to perform athletically has seen considerable growth in recent years. Everywhere you look – from newspapers and magazines to online influencers – there's advice on how we should train according to our menstrual cycle. But is the robust scientific evidence there even now?

I search the scientific journals for recent meta-analyses – studies that group a number of smaller studies together to create a larger and more robust one – looking at the effects of the menstrual cycle on female athletes. I find several, all of which conclude that, while it's possible the menstrual cycle could have some effects on performance, perception of effort and discomfort, and recovery, these are small and vary greatly between individuals. Additionally, these effects are likely to disappear altogether for anyone on hormonal contraception.

The analyses also raise concerns about both the overall quality of the original research carried out and the effect of simply believing that various phases of the menstrual cycle might make us better or worse at sport. I find myself surprised by how little concrete evidence there is for all the headlines, advice and apps that have proliferated in the wake of some small, preliminary research findings.

As with so many other areas of women's lives in which we're told that our physiology is in some way letting us down, there's clearly money to be made. Good-quality research studies and dissemination of findings are essential to enabling women to reach their potential in sport safely, sustainably and effectively. But currently, in this area of research, the evidence remains far from clear.

* * *

I first started running regularly in my mid-20s, after a car crash in Italy left me with a fractured spine and collar bone, unable to walk for several weeks. It was a powerful reminder of the privilege of having a body that worked, and I vowed to look after it better than I had done before. Recovery was slow, but eventually I could run again. A mile around the block became two, and soon I'd progressed into running half marathons and then marathons.

At the time, Paula Radcliffe was dominating women's marathon running and was a huge inspiration to me. This was before social media, so I absorbed every detail I could about how she lived, trained, ate and slept from magazines like *Runner's World* and *Athletics Weekly*. I would pore over articles, photos and footage, admiring her drive to succeed and utter dedication to her sport. I cried with her when her 2004 Olympic marathon in Athens ended with her sitting on a kerb due to stomach trouble. Despite being one of the world's greatest ever marathon runners and representing Great Britain at four consecutive Olympics from 1996 to 2008, Paula never won an Olympic medal.

While she was light years better than I was at running, I saw Paula as similar enough to me to allow myself to dream of becoming a better runner. Her successes and heartbreaks captured my imagination, motivating me to push myself harder – to be just a little more like her. Paula's influence shaped me, showing me it was possible for women to be strong and fast, cultivating a lifelong, deep love for running. This experience lives with me today as a reminder of the importance and power of representation – of seeing people we perceive as similar to ourselves, whether that's our gender, age, race, body or any other factor we can latch on to and think, 'If they can do it, then so can I.'

Eventually, the boredom and injuries resulting from many miles of running on tarmac pushed me to look for alternatives to the marathon. I began to take my first tentative steps off-road, finding the terrain frustrating and slow to run on at first, while my body and brain adapted, but also relishing the sense of freedom and adventure. My first off-road race was the 32-kilometre (20-mile) Axe to Exe. It was 2004, and the first year the race had been held, tracing the Jurassic Coast between Seaton and Exmouth in Devon. I had never run anything like it before, so I raced it like a marathon, going out too hard and trying to hang on. By the end, I was sick and hallucinating but absolutely sold on this new kind of running. Once I had recovered, I knew I didn't want to go back to the roads. 20 years later, the Axe to Exe is still going strong and I'll be forever grateful for the introduction to big adventures on the trails it gave me.

Off-road running, and in particular fell and hill running, has a long history in northern Britain, originating in the early 19th century when shepherds and farm workers would race each other across the 'fells' – local hills and mountains. Fell races, often held at rural fairs, remain a celebration of both community and landscape, with the fittest, fastest and strongest battling it out for the win. The fells of Northern England were also home to some of the earliest ultramarathons that allowed women to compete. The Fellsman, a 96 kilomtre (60 mile) race in the Yorkshire Dales, and the Lake District 4 x 3,000 race both permitted women to enter as early as the 1960s.

Like most people in the south of the UK, I grew up knowing nothing about fell running. But the same year I ran the Axe to Exe, Richard Askwith's book, *Feet in the Clouds: A Tale of Fell Running and Obsession*, changed everything. Capturing the imagination of many – myself included – the book explores the world of fell running: its culture, characters and Askwith's personal goal – to complete the Bob Graham Round, a 106-kilometre (66-mile), 27,000-feet circuit of 42 of the highest peaks in the English Lake District within 24 hours. *Feet in the Clouds* also introduced me to some of fell running's greatest women, including Angela Mudge, Helene Whitaker (née Diamantides), Wendy Dodds and Pauline Stuart. These women were tough, muscled and agile, powering through mud and moving goat-like over mountains. I was hooked. I had discovered a new world of running, far removed from the roads, and I couldn't get enough of it.

The year after *Feet in the Clouds* was published, British runner Nicky Spinks completed her first Bob Graham Round. The following year, at the age of 38, she was diagnosed with breast cancer, undergoing treatment, including a mastectomy. While many advised her to rest, running was an important part of Nicky's coping and recovery strategy, and over the years she would go on to break new ground in women's mountain ultrarunning. In 2012, she set a new women's Bob Graham Round record of 18:12, lowering this to 18:06 in 2015. During this time, she also set the women's records for the Paddy Buckley Round in

Wales and the Ramsay Round in Scotland, simultaneously holding the women's fastest times for all three British 24-hour mountain rounds. Her record would stand until 2016, when it was beaten by another legend of the fell and ultrarunning scene, Jasmin Paris. Incredibly, Nicky would also go on to run *double* rounds between 2016 and 2019. The first of these, the double Bob Graham Round, covered a distance of 212 kilometres (132 miles) with more than 54,000 feet of ascent. It was, Nicky said at the time, a celebration of still being alive and running, 10 years after her cancer diagnosis and treatment.

'It has changed my perspective on things and made me do challenges as soon as I can, and to appreciate it that much more,' she told the *Guardian* in an interview in 2016. 'Being told I had cancer was hard to deal with – there are not many things worse – and that keeps me going through the races when I'm struggling.'

* * *

At the same time as fell running was becoming established in Britain, the late 1800s were a time of relative freedom for women in the outdoors – for wealthy white women, at least. In her book *In Her Nature*, Rachel Hewitt traces the life of Lizzie Le Blond, an Irish Alpinist, author and photographer who documented women participating in tobogganing, skiing and mountaineering in the Alps during the late 1800s and founded the Ladies' Alpine Club. Lizzie's passion and work forged a place for women in an arena traditionally dominated by men; but men also featured strongly in her life, teaching her the skills she required to be competent and safe and guiding her on climbs.

Incredibly, the world of women's ultradistance sport was also thriving at this time, with increasing numbers of women participating in pedestrianism – competitive long-distance footraces that gained unexpected popularity as a spectator sport. Six-day races experienced an explosion in popularity in both the US and UK during this time. Why six days? Because competitive sport was not permitted on Sundays.

Of the 850 total starters across 85 6-day races that took place during 1879, at least 120 were women, with 17 women's-only races taking place. That year, the first women's international 6-day race was held in Madison Square Garden, New York. It would be the first 'go-as-you-please' race for women – meaning that running was permitted. For the first time in women's ultradistance competition, big prize money was on offer, with $1,000 (equivalent to about $28,000/£22,000 in today's money) for the winner, along with a belt made by Tiffany, worth around $250. The entry fee was $200, but any woman who completed more than 350 miles would have their fee refunded.

Many pedestriennes were extremely poor and had few choices or opportunities. Some were single mothers, while some others were in abusive, coercive relationships with husbands or managers. The ability to keep moving for hours and days was a skill they could use to make money, a talent borne from the hardships they endured in everyday life.

Eighteen women started the race, many wearing heavy velvet skirts and some sporting dancing shoes, completely inadequate for the demands of long-distance running and quickly filling with sawdust from the track. The women made their way around the track accompanied by jeers and taunts from men in the crowd, some of whom even followed them to loiter around their sleeping area.

As the days passed, most competitors dropped out due to injury, lack of training and/or lack of food. By the start of day six, only five women remained in the race, of whom three had established a clear lead: Bertha Von Berg, a boot and shoe seamstress from New York, who had a 100-mile time of 23 hours; Bella Kilbury from New Jersey, who, at 16, was the youngest in the race; and 30-year-old Ada Wallace from Maryland, who had covered 100 miles in 24 hours earlier that year. During the sixth and final day, Kilbury, who had been in third place, overtook Wallace to move into second. Furious, Wallace began hurling insults and threats of physical violence at the younger woman, who had to be escorted for her own protection. In the end, Von Berg set a new world record of 372 miles, with Kilbury holding on to her second place with 351 miles and Wallace finishing third with 336 miles.

The 1870s also saw 100-mile races take off, with vast crowds of paying spectators turning up to cheer on walkers and runners who circled for hours and hours. US-based races were strictly heel–toe walking only; but, as the decade progressed, British races permitted running as well as walking, resulting in increasingly fast times over the distance. At this time, according to ultrarunning historian Davy Crockett, the Royal Agricultural Hall (now Islington Business Design Centre) was the ultrarunning capital of the world.

In his 2022 book on Britain's celebrated pedestriennes, *Pioneers in Bloomers*, Rob Hadgraft tells the story of Kate Wiltshire (née Rider), a relative of former New Zealand Prime Minister Jacinda Ardern. Leaving domestic service in London in 1872, Kate travelled unaccompanied on an immigrant ship to New Zealand with the aim of starting a new life. En route, she fell in love with another emigrant, Joe, and the couple married the following year, a week before Kate's 20th birthday. A successful long-distance walker in England, Joe brought the sport to New Zealand, and also to Kate, who proved to be a prodigious talent.

In 1876, at a time when few men had covered 100 miles in under 24 hours, and it was therefore considered an impossible feat for women, a crowd gathered at Auckland's City Hall to watch Kate make her attempt at the distance. The aim was to cover 100 miles – 2,833 laps of a 62-yard indoor track – in 24 hours. Dressed in a much talked-about colourful outfit, and accompanied by the Artillery Band, she set off on the evening of Friday, 5th May to much initial enthusiasm, which gradually waned as the hours passed.

Throughout the night and the following day, she continued her 62-yard circles, the crowds returning in force to see her finish the following evening. Despite an interruption from a drunken sailor, and badly twisting her ankle in the early hours of the morning, Kate Wiltshire was hailed as the first woman to complete 100 miles on foot in under 24 hours, crossing the line in around 23 hours and 40 minutes. Her sporting prowess would be remembered by her great-great-granddaughter, Prime Minister Ardern, in her speech when taking office in 2017.

By 1878, the most popular 100-mile races were women's races. German pedestrienne Bertha Von Hillern's training involved walking for 4 hours every day and spending an hour on gym exercises. Her exhibition 100-milers took 27–28 hours and drew large crowds. Between 1877 and 1878, Von Hillern was the most prolific 100-mile racer, man or woman, covering the distance at least 12 times during a 12-month period. She also revolutionized women's walking footwear, competing in shoes with little or no heel – which was shocking for the time.

Women gradually disappeared from long-distance running competitions in the early 20th century. However, Geraldine Watson, a teacher from South Africa, was known to walk up to 200 miles at a time, carrying an automatic pistol for protection. In 1931, she ran the 54-mile Comrades Marathon unofficially, finishing in just over 11 hours. In 1933, she reduced this time to 9 hours 31 minutes. She was the last woman to run the race until 1965. In 1934, she ran a road 100-miler in Durban in 22 hours 22 minutes. Only two men finished ahead of her.

It wasn't until the 1970s that women began competing in 6-day and 100-mile races once more, but still with some opposition from governing bodies – the Amateur Athletics Union (AAU) banned women from competitions. However, most ultramarathons were not regulated by the AAU and allowed women to run.

In 1970, Japanese American Miki Gorman set a new women's 100-mile record of 21 hours, 4 minutes and 4 seconds. Miki went on to win the New York and Boston city marathons twice and ran a personal best of 2 hours 39; but she never competed at the Olympic Games as the women's marathon was not included until after her career had ended.

Another female ultrarunning pioneer at this time was Californian Natalie Cullimore. A former cyclist, in 1970, at the age of 34 and just 2 months after her first-ever race, she won the National 50 Miles Championship with a time of 7:35:57, setting an American women's record. The following year, Cullimore set a new women's 100-mile record at the Camellia 100 in Rocklin, California. The only woman in a field of 17 runners, she came in first overall in a time of 16:11:00. Two years later, at a 100-mile race in Sacramento, California, she again took the overall win, finishing in 18:09:16 and beating the first man by more than 4 hours.

British runner Eleanor Robinson also discovered her hidden talents in the 1970s and 80s. After leaving school and getting married, she trained as a PE teacher and became, in her words, a 'closet runner' because it wasn't seen as socially acceptable for married women to be out running. She risked being shouted at if she was seen running alone, so she would wait until after dark before heading out. As the running boom of the 1980s took hold, and the idea of women being out running became more accepted, Eleanor started taking her running more seriously.

Her first marathon, in her early 30s as a mum of three, was the People's Marathon for fun runners in Birmingham in 1981, three years before the women's marathon was included in the Olympic Games. Training in the evenings once the children were in bed, and with a longest run of 18 kilometres (11 miles), she finished second in a time of 3:24. The following year, she improved her marathon time to 3:09, which would be the last time she ran more than 3 hours for a marathon before the age of 50. But it was in the long and really long races that Eleanor would shine brightest: she went on to set more than 30 world records across distances from 48 kilometres (30 miles) to 6 days and achieved 6 world titles.

In 1983, Eleanor was the only woman to take part in the first ever running of the Spartathlon race, a 245-kilometre (152-miles) ultramarathon from Athens to Sparta in Greece. She recalls the difficulty she had being accepted into the race. The organizers were strongly opposed to women running the race, and it was only after some of the male ultrarunners intervened that Eleanor was allowed to compete, leaving her with no time to train specifically for the race.

Despite the lack of preparation, however, Eleanor finished ninth overall, beating many well-regarded male ultrarunners. In an interview with Katie Holmes, from the website runyoung50.co.uk, which boasts a wonderful wealth of detail on the history of women's running, Eleanor says of blazing a trail for the many women who have since run Spartathlon: 'I was always very conscious of being a pioneer and that was one of the motivating factors for me. I was well aware of the fact that there were very few women [doing ultrarunning] and that I was fortunate in that I was around at the right time and able to take the opportunities. I was doing it not just for me but for other women that might want to. I knew it wasn't the sort of thing that would attract hordes of people, but it would make the way easier for anybody else that wanted to come along and do similar things.'

Since the return of women to 100-mile running, less than 50 years ago, the records have almost halved. At the time of writing, US ultrarunner Camille Herron's astonishing road (12:41:11), track (12:52:50) and trail (12:42:40) records are testament to what's possible if women are given the opportunity to train and race consistently, blazing a trail of hope for those who follow.

And yet, as I explore the history of women's ultrarunning, unearthing stories of women achieving incredible feats of endurance in the late 19th and 20th centuries, I wonder why it feels like we're still breaking new ground, even now. Why does it so often seem like women have to fight to get to start lines?

2

BREAKING BARRIERS

'I think that all sounds completely sensible in the crazy
world of ultrarunning.'

—Courtney Dauwalter, multiple
race winner and record holder

As I research the history and science of running
100 miles, one thing becomes very clear: it takes
months, and even years, of highly specific training
and preparation to ensure both body and mind are ready to
cope with the demands of keeping going for such a long way.
I realize how long it's been since I last did any structured
training, look at suggested training times and volumes, and
wonder how I'll fit it all in.

Daily life is busy – from the moment I get out of bed at
5am to fit in a couple of hours' work before the kids wake
up, to reading them their bedtime stories at the end of the
day. In between work, which Sim and I do from our tiny
office at home, I still run most days; but these runs are often
squeezed into any available time and might include several

stops to answer emails along the way. Rather than being something I do as a means of training for a specific goal or race, running, for the past decade or more, has simply been an escape: precious time to myself, to stretch my legs, free my mind, enjoy the local scenery and wildlife and remind myself there are other people in the world.

In theory, becoming a better runner is easy. Improvements in fitness follow the progressive overload principle, in which stresses are applied to the various systems of the body during training, creating short-term imbalances. The body, governed by homeostasis – the requirement to keep its internal conditions within a fairly narrow range to maintain optimal function – restores these imbalances through chemical and hormonal means. Apply too much stress at once and the imbalances become too great to restore, resulting in damage – usually burnout, illness or injury. Allow too little time between stressors and you get the same thing. Apply too little stress, however, and no adaptation occurs, meaning you don't get fitter.

Adaptations to exercise-induced stresses are also highly specific. If you're training to run a fast 5 kilometres (3 miles), you'll need to include plenty of fast running in your training, stimulating the specific adaptations required for fast-5k running. Anyone who's trained for a marathon knows how important the long runs are; covering 32 kilometres (20 miles) and more multiple times before race day is essential. These long runs stimulate the adaptations required for marathon running, which include everything from muscle strength and fatigue resistance; changes to the cardiovascular system to ensure that sufficient oxygen- and nutrient-rich blood is delivered to working muscles over several hours of running; the ability to eat and drink on the run; and the psychological skills to keep going when you really want to stop.

Training for shorter ultras – up to about 100 kilometres (62 miles) – isn't that different to training for marathons. At the longer end of this range, it's probably a good idea to include some runs longer than 32 kilometres (20 miles), but many runners who successfully complete these distances don't. At the point at which I decide to run 100 miles, I've run 100 kilometres twice – both times at Race to the Stones, which traces the course of England's oldest road, the Ridgeway, through Oxfordshire and Wiltshire – and, while it was of course difficult, at no point did I think I couldn't finish. A hundred miles, though . . . that feels like an entirely different beast, adding another 60 kilometres (40 miles) to the furthest I've ever run. This would take me upwards of 24 hours and through at least one night.

I wonder whether I should follow a training plan, scrolling through a few on various websites. But they're all too rigid and generic, and I know with so many other demands on my time any fixed plan will only set me up for failure. Then I think about all those women who inspired me to take on this challenge, who've run many 100-milers and learned by experience what works and what doesn't. And I realize that *that*'s where I need to look for advice. These are the women who will understand what I'll go through over the coming months and why I want to put myself through it. And if I want to run just a little more like them, I'll need to train, eat, sleep and think a little more like them. I'll need to live the life of the ultrarunning women I so admire. I want to delve deeper into their stories – their experiences and motivations – and through them find a way that works for me. And who better to start with than the woman widely considered the best female ultrarunner of all time, Courtney Dauwalter.

The first time I speak with Courtney, she looks just like she always does – hair swept back into a bun, big smile, blue eyes that constantly seem to be searching for answers.

'Hi Courtney!' I say, trying not to fangirl too obviously.

'I can't hear you,' she says.

I must have hosted a hundred Zoom interviews since the COVID-19 pandemic moved our lives online, and this is the first time I've ever had sound issues. I click on my microphone, change some settings, panic and then write in the chat that I'll need to log back in on my phone. Then Courtney disappears. I can't believe it. One chance to interview the world's most famous female ultrarunner and I've messed it up.

Eventually, I manage to get everything working and nervously begin making my way through my list of questions. But I needn't have worried. Courtney's lovely – helpful, passionate, enthusiastic and completely without ego despite her fame and achievements. I explain my project to her – that I'm researching women's ultrarunning and am toying with the idea of running 100 miles myself.

'That's very cool,' she says. 'I'm pumped for you to try 100 miles – it's such a fun distance.'

When I tell her about some of the races I've looked at and my worries about running an ultra in notoriously unpredictable British weather, Courtney laughs. 'You wouldn't want to not get the full adventure – you want the whole thing!' she tells me. It's something I've learned about Courtney from watching and listening to her past interviews: there's always a positive. However dark, dreadful and painful a running experience is, she always manages to find something awesome in it; always wants to discover more – about the trail, about enduring, about what her mind can make her body do. Perhaps this is one of her biggest strengths when it comes to doing what she does.

Her enthusiasm is infectious. It helps me to reframe my thoughts about undertaking a 100-miler – to focus on the challenge and the excitement rather than the fear.

'When I stumbled into the ultrarunning world, every time I signed up for a new distance I was certain it would kill me. And when it ended up not killing me it made me think, "What's the next thing that's possible?" From the get-go I was curious – I'd think, "Well I've done this distance so now I have to try this next distance because it sounds insane, and that's the place I want to put myself." I wanted those adventures, and I wanted the challenge, and I wanted to try the thing that sounded impossible.'

Courtney had run races of 50 kilometres and 50 miles before she signed up for her first 100-mile race. She'd wanted to pick one that would be an adventure and opted for the Run Rabbit Run race in the Colorado Mountains.

'I knew there'd be plenty of climbing, temperature changes – the full adventure package,' she says.

But her first attempt at 100 miles didn't go to plan. She describes how, as the hours went on, her body hurt more and more.

'Instead of thinking that was normal, my brain immediately went into panic mode. Around mile 50 I started telling myself that if my legs and feet and body hurt this much this early on, I must not be cut out for 100 miles. There was a voice telling me that I couldn't finish this and that it was a joke that I'd signed up for it – like, super negative. By mile 60 I had just convinced myself that I wasn't going to make it to the finish line and that I should drop out. At the mile-70 aid station they cut my wristband and I was out of the race. In hindsight, it was all mental; something I didn't understand yet.'

This brain–body connection is what draws Courtney to ultrarunning and what keeps her signing up for the long races.

'We need to understand how important what we tell ourselves and what our mindset is when things get difficult.'

Dropping out of that race was a powerful learning experience for Courtney. The aid station she'd dropped out at was remote, so she'd had to sit and watch the runners – runners who were doing the same thing she'd been doing – coming through as they, too, tried to run 100 miles.

'It was clear they were hurting. That their legs and feet were hurting. But they were keeping going. So, I had this really concrete evidence that the thing I'd been experiencing was okay, and normal, and that I could have kept pushing through. That night, I sat at that aid station and watched how people kept moving, and what they did at aid stations. It was like having a front-row seat in the classroom of ultrarunning. The next day I was pretty disappointed, and already scheming how I would attack this distance next time; what I needed to change and do better. I decided I wanted to be someone who could run 100 miles.'

Looking back on it, Courtney's grateful for that experience, as it helped her understand just how important the brain is in ultrarunning.

'From then onwards, I knew that you couldn't go down that negative whirlpool in your head; that you have to work on different strategies to help you keep moving.'

Even Courtney still has moments when negativity and doubt creep in, though. I ask her how she manages those times; what keeps her going when everything's screaming at her to stop.

'In those moments when everything's hurting and I've been pushing through for many hours and it would be so much easier to just stop, that's when I intentionally flip the script in my head to something more neutral or positive.

Or I remind myself that those hard moments are the reason I sign up for these races.'

She tells me about her experience at Grand Raid de la Réunion, also known as Diagonale des Fous – the crazy crossing – a notoriously tough and mountainous 166-kilometre (103-mile) race on Réunion Island during which she really struggled with thoughts of stopping.

'In that moment, I said out loud to myself: "This is what you came for – to struggle, to hurt, and to find new ways to push through." To reframe this visit to the pain cave as a celebration and the reason I'm doing this race as opposed to trying to avoid it.'

Courtney often talks about using mantras to get through the hard times, with some of her favourites being, 'You're fine, this is fine, everything's fine,' and, 'Be patient, be brave, believe.' When she feels her thoughts are running too far ahead, thinking about how far away the finish or the next aid station is, she'll remind herself to stay where her feet are.

For me, this is an interesting contrast to the notion of 'chunking' in sport psychology – the idea that you can break dauntingly longer distances down into shorter chunks, focusing on getting to the next aid station, or even the next tree. But, as Courtney says, when you're really hurting even the next tree can feel like a long way, so staying right where your feet are – just taking the next step, and then the next – can help get you through.

The concept of the pain cave isn't a new one, but it's become Courtney's speciality. Each race is an opportunity to visit the cave, to explore, redecorate and chip away at it to make it – and therefore her capacity for endurance – bigger. She doesn't shy away from pain, or even try to reframe pain as something else, as some athletes and sport psychologists do. Instead, she makes it something other than herself. The pain isn't her, or hers – it's a different entity; a cave in which she is dwelling during the hard times of a race – a cave that gives her choices. She can leave the pain cave whenever she chooses to do so; and it's perhaps because of this that she's able to keep going in, to discover and actively create new depths.

I speak with Courtney in November 2022, after a year in which she'd set a new course record at Hardrock 100 in Colorado, US. But 2023 will be even more impressive. Starting out with a win and new course record at Transgrancanaria in March, she'll go on to win the Bandera 100k (62 miles) in Texas, USA, securing her one of the coveted Golden Ticket entries for that year's Western States 100-miler in California. At Western States in June, she sets a new course record of 15:29:33, finishing first woman and sixth overall. Canada-based British runner Ellie Greenwood's 2012 course record of 16:47:19 had, until then, been considered untouchable. Three weeks later, Courtney runs the Hardrock 100, finishing first woman and fourth overall in a new record time of 26:14:12, beating her own record from the previous year by 30 minutes. Just a month later, at the Ultra-Trail du Mont Blanc (UTMB) in Europe in September, she'll again take the win in the women's race.

It's an astonishing feat – and a triple crown no other ultrarunner has achieved – driven by her insatiable curiosity for what's possible, for where her limits lie. I wonder whether she's answered that question – for now, at least. Recovery from her 2023 season involves pacing her husband, Kevin, at the Swiss Alps 100k and running the Javelina Jundred 100k in Arizona, USA, with her mum – both women wearing Shortneys – the long, baggy shorts Courtney's sponsor Salomon have created for her. She hopes these shorts will give women an alternative to the current offerings – which I've often lamented are always shorter and always tighter than the men's versions.

Courtney and her husband Kevin are the ultimate team. He's 'the spreadsheet guy' who does the planning; crewing and pacing her at races and keeping her spirits up with (often terrible) jokes. Courtney rarely shows or offers vulnerability or intimate details, and her approaches to both training and diet are based on feel rather than prescription or fad. In public, she's almost always smiling; she won't be drawn into controversy and she never expresses anything other than insatiable positivity and curiosity when asked for her thoughts on . . . almost anything. In this era of oversharing, when social media can be such a difficult, opinionated and triggering arena, she's mastered the art of protecting both herself and others.

Now she's in her later 30s, Courtney's strength and speed in ultrarunning seem only to be getting better. But her journey into endurance sport started early, supported by her parents and following in the footsteps of her two older brothers – who she credits for the baggy tees and shorts that have become her trademark. Growing up in Minnesota, she competed in track, cross-country and Nordic skiing, becoming four-time Minnesota state champion in Nordic skiing. She credits this time as being foundational for her ultrarunning career – not just in developing a resilient body, but also, through her coaches, learning to embrace and manage pain and knowing that, in endurance sport, you always have more to give.

After saying goodbye to Courtney, I'm left with a sense of having spoken to someone truly unique, forging her own path in the way she knows works best for her. It's a sentiment I'm determined to take into my training and racing as I work towards my own 100-mile goal.

* * *

It's July and Southern England is in the grip of a heatwave. My local trails, usually densely lush and a riot of green, have been baked into mile upon mile of bare, cracked earth and yellow grass. Glossy black rooks amble about, beaks gaping to cool themselves down. The river looks sluggish, and lower than I've ever seen it before. As I get ready for my run – nothing more spectacular than an easy 10 kilometres (6 miles), but which I've decided marks the official start of 100-mile training – I'm aware of nerves somewhere. Strange.

As I plug my running watch in to charge it, I realize I can't remember the last time I ran with a fixed goal in mind. I haven't used a watch of any kind for years, preferring not to be tethered by the wrist, but for the coming weeks and months I'll need to know how far I'm covering and with how much ascent. I've a vague idea how fast I was running when I trained for marathons and half-marathons in the past – the minutes per mile I'd expect to hit for runs that felt easy, moderate, hard and all-out – so the watch will give me an indication of where my fitness lies now by comparison. I strap it on and feel the discomfort of its unaccustomed weight – a weight of expectation as much as its physical heft. I fiddle with it throughout this first run, trying to get it to feel comfortable, misunderstanding where the true discomfort is coming from.

The general busy nature of life and work has meant I've not run as much as usual over the past months. With running having been so relaxed and unstructured, my loss of fitness hasn't been particularly obvious. But now, as I look with dismay at the numbers on my watch, it becomes painfully so. My pace is well below where I expected it to be and my heart rate is far higher.

With the watch as my guide, I am amazed at how hard running feels – slow and lethargic, like I'm moving through treacle. The numbers crawl interminably by, but I can't give up yet. I push on, desperately wanting to stop. The heat is oppressive, the air windless and humid. My heartbeat whooshes in my ears, my face fiery with the heat. Focusing on the trail ahead, I try to ignore the river; try to block out how cool and inviting it looks, meandering serenely through the parched countryside. It's low, but I know there are places that still hold enough water to swallow my whole body, cold and deep and soothing. Later, I promise myself. Later . . .

At long last, the watch reads 10 kilometres and I stop dead, refusing to go another step. Sod the cooldown; there's no cooling down in this weather. I sit down at the side of the trail and wait for my stressed body to return to a state that feels more normal. Usually, my post-run emotion lies somewhere between satisfaction and elation, but today I mostly feel like crying. Instead, I strip down to my sports bra and running shorts and slip gratefully into the cool, brown depths of the river.

By the end of the first week of trying to train to the dictates of my watch, several distinct thoughts have emerged. Firstly, I'm not enjoying it. I've been running for the pure love of running for years, heading out aimlessly and joyfully into the wildlife-filled, trail-rich countryside that surrounds our home. For the past week, though, I have ploughed up and down the towpath with my eyes fixed on the numbers – usually the wrong numbers – on my wrist. The thought of my daily run has been stress-inducing, not exciting. Usually, I firmly believe that age is just a number; that I am fitter and stronger than many people half my age. But this approach to training is just making me feel old and unfit. This might be the quickest and most effective way to achieve the best fitness of my life – but if I'm not enjoying it, what's the point?

I think back to my conversation with Courtney, her free-spirited and intuitive approach to training, and I make a decision: I will not let my watch dictate how I feel about running. I know it will be important to know how far I've run, and over how much ascent; but from now on I will base the effort of my runs on how I feel, not what my watch tells me. And I will let love, not numbers, be my motivation.

* * *

Something I've noticed as women's ultrarunning achievements have become more regular and recognized is that people do care about it. In 2019, Jasmin Paris, a vet, research scientist and mum of two from the UK, shot to global fame after she became the first woman to claim the overall win at the UK's Montane Winter Spine Race. Widely regarded as among the world's toughest ultras, the Spine Race covers more than 418 kilometres (260 miles) between Edale in the Peak District and Kirk Yetholm in the Scottish Borders. Running through the cold, dark and mud of the British winter, runners cross the Yorkshire Dales, Hadrian's Wall and the Cheviot Hills, carrying their own kit for the entirety of the race. Jasmin crossed the finish line in 83:12:23, beating the course record by 12 hours and the previous women's record by 24 hours, all while expressing milk for her 14-month-old daughter along the way. Incredibly, Jasmin had gone home, showered, slept, and appeared on BBC *Breakfast* before the second-placed runner and first man, Eoin Keith, finished 15 hours later.

When I speak with Jasmin in 2023, she talks modestly about her achievements, about how fitting training in around a full-time job as a clinical academic and being a mum of two young children means getting up at five every morning.

We share stories of running and breastfeeding; noting how, for ultrarunning mums, breastfeeding is just another part of the logistical puzzle of running and racing that needs to be fitted in. For Jasmin, the platform she was afforded by this unexpected publicity is important for showing other mums what is possible, as well as demanding more specific support for women at such events.

This is something I discuss with Penny Welch and Nick Tuppen, CCO and CEO respectively at Threshold Sports. Long-term friends and colleagues, and both former high-level rowers, they're clearly passionate about bringing ultrarunning to more people. As Nick puts it, it's not just a good business decision for them. Demonstrating that it's possible to organize races in a way that's accessible and welcoming to a diverse range of runners – including spending time and money on getting the important things right for those who experience the most barriers to participation – can be a sustainable business model. Rather than cutting corners, Threshold made the decision to drop one of its races from its ultra series because it wasn't possible to deliver the level of support they wanted to within budget.

I was still breastfeeding the first time I ran Race to the Stones, one of Threshold's 100-kilometre races. But it hadn't even crossed my mind to arrange for Sim to bring our baby son along to the aid stations so I could feed him en route – something that would have made the day easier and more enjoyable for all of us. In my naivete, neither had I considered expressing milk along the way. As a result, by the time

I reached the finish I was sporting two enormous, rock-solid, watermelon-like boobs. It was incredibly uncomfortable, but entirely down to my poor planning. At least I was completely distracted from the pain in my legs.

Having (to my mind) erred quite badly on that first attempt, I returned to Race to the Stones a few years later, post breastfeeding, and had a fantastic run. My memories are of plenty of toilets, lots of choice of food and drink, smiling and incredibly helpful staff and a route that lent itself well to simply focusing on running, rather than having too much in the way of navigational or terrain-related challenges. During my conversation with Penny and Nick, I share my watermelon-boobs story and they laugh. But we then discuss more seriously the need to ensure there's provision for those who want to breastfeed or express milk along the way.

Since my first attempt at Race to the Stones, many more women have publicly shared their experiences of running long distances while breastfeeding, demonstrating that it's absolutely possible to choose to breastfeed *and* take on huge endurance challenges. For Jasmin, who chose to continue breastfeeding into her daughter's second year – as I did with my children – the need to express milk during her winning, record-breaking run was a simple, practical consideration alongside everything else required to run a multi-day winter ultramarathon. Grippy shoes – tick. Waterproof jacket with taped seams – tick. Emergency survival bag – tick. Breast pump – tick. I just love that mindset.

Like me, Penny is a mid-40s mum, emerging from the all-encompassing state of mothering young children into a place of possibility. Having trained so hard and competed to such a high level in the past, before having children, she also knows what it feels like to push her limits. In 2023, she took part in one of Threshold's 50k (31-mile) events, walking it with two of her friends, completing it in 10 hours and having a great time along the way. I'm intrigued to learn how the reality of the experience compared with her expectations. Had the things she'd been concerned about come up?

'I actually think I found it easier than I expected to,' she tells me after a momentary pause to consider. 'It wasn't easy – but it was nowhere near as hard as I'd worried it might be.'

I probably get a bit overexcited at this. It's the message I've heard so many times from women – particularly older women and particularly mums, for whom daily life is often such hard work that spending a day or two running, chatting, being looked after and offered food and cups of tea, can feel a bit like a holiday; well worth enduring some prolonged running- or walking-related discomfort for. We all admire those who undertake big, hard endurance challenges. We watch their struggles unfold, applaud them as they cross the finish line, having battled the weather, the terrain and the discomfort, and hand them medals to recognize their achievements. But perhaps the real heroes are those who've already been at the finish line for hours, waiting for the triumphal return and managing the kids in the meantime.

Threshold's Ultra 50:50 campaign aims to achieve gender parity on the start line. Having got close to this figure prior to the COVID-19 pandemic, they've noticed that male participation rates have returned to pre-pandemic levels while women's have not. Worryingly, this is a trend mirrored across the sector, and highlighted in Sport England's annual Active Lives Survey 2023. According to the results, the gender gap in sports participation is now at 5 per cent – the largest it has been since reporting began. Breaking down these figures by ethnicity, the gap becomes even more stark. While 5 per cent fewer white women in Britain participate in sport compared with white men, this gap doubles for Asian women and rises still further – to 11 per cent – for black women.

When I dig deeper into the numbers, it's clear that gender disparity in sport starts very early on for girls. In terms of primary-age children, only 30 per cent of parents think playing sport is very important for their daughters compared to 41 per cent of parents for their sons. But it's also clear that having sporty parents is one of the biggest drivers of sports participation in children: 82 per cent of girls aged 5 to 11 who have parents who love sport also love sport themselves, compared to 59 per cent of girls with parents who don't like sport. For me, this is an important one. Mum guilt over spending time doing sports-related activities is a huge reason why many of the women I've spoken to struggle to do as much as they'd like; yet being a sporty female role model is probably the biggest gift we can give our daughters to ensure they grow up loving and taking part in sport.

Anna Troup's numerous ultrarunning achievements include wins at the 268-mile Summer Spine race, Lakeland 100 and Arc of Attrition 100. Having often been part of Anna's support team at races, at the age of 16 Anna's daughter Milly joined her mum to run the Javelina Jundred (pronounced Havelina Hundred) – a 100 race through Arizona's Fountain Hills. While some question running such a long way at such a young age (governing body British Athletics states a minimum age of 20 for ultramarathon competitors) Milly only seems to have taken positives from it. When I speak with her in 2023, she's in the midst of a university degree, and tells me how powerful the experience of training for and completing 100 miles has been, giving her confidence that she can do hard things, even in areas far removed from running. When things are difficult – in life or in her degree – she can look back on that experience and draw strength and resilience from it.

The absence of women in many sporting arenas is a vicious circle for many women and girls, who never have their interest piqued because they don't see themselves represented. Instead, they see themselves as either not welcome or, worse, not capable. This is even more so for women and girls of colour.

Renee McGregor is a mum, author and sports dietician who has been a friend and running buddy for the past six years. Before she moved to the Lake District to fulfil some of her mountain-running dreams, we lived just a few minutes' run from each other and shared many miles on our local trails. We're similar in many ways, being women and mothers in our 40s, writers, working in sport and having a love of running and mountains. But there's one way in which we differ, and that shapes our experiences – especially within arenas such as outdoor sport – in very different ways: our skin colour.

Despite having spent hundreds of hours chatting – or 'putting the world to rights', as she calls it – I've never really heard Renee talking in detail about her experiences of being a woman of colour in the arena of ultrarunning before. It's rare, in fact, for us to sit down and talk about any one subject – usually our conversations involve being slightly out of breath, keeping half an eye on our dogs and wondering if we've taken a wrong turning. But I'm really pleased she's keen to talk about this now, and wants to share a message far and wide – even though it's at times uncomfortable for her – because she knows how much difference it will make to others, including her two daughters.

'Sometimes it's hard keeping going, and I know both Sabrina [Pace Humphreys – founder of Black Trail Runners and author of *Black Sheep: A Story of Rural Racism, Identity and Hope*] and I get to this point where we feel like we can't do this any more – can't put out any more fires. But it's all we can do, so we keep going. I think we just need to keep talking about it, and it is being talked about more, so it's working. Even though it's taking time, we are seeing change – it's small but it's good change. Maybe there won't be real change in my mum's lifetime, or even in mine, but we are effecting change, and our daughters are getting the benefit of that.'

Renee's parents immigrated to the UK from India in the 1960s and she grew up living above their shop on a council estate. Her earliest memories of school involve being chased and bullied for her skin colour. Now she's in her late 40s but tells me that still, every day, when she's interacting with people, she has to consider whether they're treating her differently because of the way she looks. It's something that, as a woman, I can begin to relate to, but to a far lesser extent. It's when multiple factors interact – gender, ethnicity, age, socioeconomic background – that the greatest inequalities emerge.

But despite – or perhaps fuelled by – these difficulties, Renee has worked hard, built a successful business and written and published several books. And she's run some big races, including the Mustang Ultra in the Himalayas, the 50-kilometre Summer Spine Sprint and a 5-day, 250-kilometre (155-mile) winter race that she organized and on which I joined her for a couple of days. Her plans for the future include taking on the formidable Dragon's Back in Wales.

'I think it takes a certain type of person to override social expectations,' she tells me. 'And I think I've always been somebody who doesn't conform. Probably because of that I've found it slightly easier to follow my heart and my passion rather than let things stop me.'

Renee took up running after her second daughter was born, as a way to find some time to herself and deal with difficult thoughts. She quickly improved and was soon running with a club and competing in races, often doing well. But, whether training or racing, she never saw anyone who looked like she did.

'I definitely wouldn't say it was seeing someone like me running that made me think, "Oh I could do that." If anything, at times I'd question whether it was something I should be doing because I just didn't see any other Indian people running, and especially Indian women. In the culture my parents came from, it's just not done.'

In fact, when researching for one of her books, Renee found that Indian women were the least represented across all sports – a fact she found mind-blowing but that didn't surprise her.

'Because when I looked around me, I never saw another Indian woman playing netball or running, or even in the gym. And while this was probably partly because of places I lived, which does have an impact, the reality is that we are really underrepresented.

'When I started doing well in running, I suddenly started wondering, "Why aren't there more Indian women running? There's nothing wrong with us." Because prior to that I'd actually wondered whether there was some physiological reason why we weren't good at running, which I know sounds silly, but that was the question I would ask myself.'

Even now, after nearly 20 years of running and racing, Renee struggles with her feelings on the start line.

'I stand there feeling really uncomfortable – like there's this massive arrow pointing at me – because I look around and there won't be a single person that looks like me on that start line. I feel like people are assuming I won't do well, because of what I look like. And then when I do OK, people seem surprised and it can be quite patronizing.'

This utter absence of representation is a barrier in its own right. One look at the advertising images of many races and they're filled with young, lean, white and usually male runners. It's not surprising, faced with this imagery, that everyone else wonders whether this is somewhere they belong.

Threshold's campaign aims to tackle women's perceived barriers to training for and participating in ultras and seeks to encourage more women to give the sport a go. These barriers include limited time, safety issues when running alone, menstrual health and female representation and perception. They're working with SheRACES, an organization set up by ultrarunner Sophie Power to make races more accessible and inclusive for women. They're also going a step further and supporting a group of women who have never run an ultra before to take part in Race to the King, a 100km in the South Downs, and to collect their feedback afterwards. When I ask what they think the biggest wins are in terms of making the sport appealing to women, Nick's answer is clear: better representation in marketing campaigns, ensuring that runners of all ages, shapes and ethnicities are pictured prominently, along with walkers; and generous cutoff times.

Elle Wood, race director at Limitless Trails, completely agrees. While her races are relatively small, they attract a good number of women, including some of the best female ultrarunners around. Set amid the beautiful Bannau Brycheiniog (Brecon Beacons), infamous training ground for the SAS, these races are tough, gruelling mountain challenges. Some are self-navigated and they're all held in exposed, upland areas, often over the winter months. If Elle wanted to, she could justifiably use all the buzzwords that abound in ultramarathon marketing – the toughest, hardest, gnarliest and so on. But she doesn't. The cutoff times allow entrants to walk the routes if they wish; and no one ever worries that they're going to be coming in once everything's been packed away and everyone's gone home. I love the photos used to advertise the races, too. These depict women and men, old and young, some in fancy dress, others caught in comedy poses out on the trail, and the overriding sense is not of off-putting difficulty but of welcoming fun.

Chrissie Wellington is a four-time Ironman triathlon World Champion, and she was a huge inspiration to me when I was getting into endurance sports in my 20s. I ask Chrissie about her thoughts on why, despite a lot of work to improve equality in men's and women's participation in both long-distance triathlon and cycling, both of which she's been instrumental in effecting a change for the better, and ultrarunning, women still make up so few of those competing. 'Women still face barriers that men don't,' she tells me. 'A lot of these are psychological barriers – so that's where having role models is so important; some are practical – women, and particularly mothers, are often less able to carve out the time necessary to train, and even if they can, there are psychological barriers that don't seem to be there for men.

'Things like safety, confidence, technical skills competence. So, we need better support in terms of female-specific coaching and training that address female physiology, psychology and skill sets to help with that. For me, an enduring frustration is the research – the research around the female athlete is so lacking – historically we've just been seen as small men with lower testosterone. For example, there's so little empirical evidence on the impact of running on pregnancy or menopause. I really think that needs to be focused upon, and the results put out there. I think those things will really help to move things forward for the future.'

3

WOMEN, BODIES AND ULTRARUNNING

'As people get older they need to ask themselves "who am I?", "what do I want?" Life is not a rehearsal! You're a long time dead, so you might as well get on and do it whilst you are alive!'
—Rosie Swale-Pope, record-breaking runner, author
of *Just a Little Run Around the World*

'The body occupies a halfway house between materiality and subjectivity, unsettling those social psychological and biological frameworks by which age and ageing are traditionally understood,' observes Chris Gilleard, a professor in psychiatry at University College London, in a recent paper for the philosophy journal *Phenomenology and the Cognitive Sciences*.

Materially, our bodies are in a state of constant flux: health and illness, breakdown and repair; a balancing act in the quiet struggle for survival. Embodied beings as we are, perhaps our minds aren't so different, inseparable even, as we live, love and age while navigating the uncertain line between darkness and light. We are both old and new, carrying so much of our past with us and yet creating and recreating ourselves as we go.

Having carried and given birth to two children; having in various accidents fractured my collarbone, spine, pelvis, femur and ribs; having run on most days for the past 20 years . . . I am only too aware of the weight of my past – the writing of my history on my body. Eyed through the lens of one who has, like all women, spent a lifetime being carefully schooled in the art of how we should look, I experience my body both objectively – the visible changes brought about by time and gravity, the right shoulder that is noticeably shorter than my left due to the overlap and fusion of snapped bones – and subjectively, in the succession of niggling aches, pains and numbness that forms my daily experience of myself. My body has become, in Gilleard's words, a series of 'normal abnormalities'. Perhaps my mind has, too: the scars run no less deep.

As a female from birth, I can expect to be, on average, shorter, weaker, slower, and (also related to my body but less obviously so) poorer than males of a similar level of health and fitness. My different sex hormones mean my muscles are smaller and produce less power; my lungs suck less oxygen out of the air and my heart pumps less of this oxygen around my body. My pelvic arrangement prioritizes childbearing over the most direct transmission of forces from my gluteal muscles to my legs. In my forties I also know that, like a classic car, I'll have lost a few horsepower simply through the ageing process. With loss of elasticity, gaps start to appear; things begin to rattle.

Over almost every test of athletic prowess, I would be expected to finish behind men and people younger than myself with a similar level of fitness. But only up to a point. The point at which things change is the portal to the world of ultradistance sport.

The world of ultrarunning is a place of uprising. It's a place where those with slightly different sets of athletic skills can flourish and even dominate. It's a place where our psychology doesn't just support our physiology, it carries it along.

At distances up to the marathon, elite male runners are between 10 and 12 per cent faster than females. At 100 miles, this percentage reduces to about 8 per cent. But it depends on the race – at the Western States in 2023, Courtney Dauwalter's time as the winning woman was only just over 3 per cent slower than that of Tom Evans, who won the men's race. The difficulty, when it comes to comparing performances over longer distances, especially when mountains and trails are concerned, is that over all those miles and all those hours of running, there are so many variables – far more than on a track or road. To compare times directly, they need to be on the same course on the same day, with the same depth of field in the women's and men's races. If we simply use retrospective data – results from the past – to make up our minds and set our expectations for the future, we're never going to capture the full complexity or exciting possibilities of this picture.

There are plenty of examples of women outperforming men by a big margin in really long, really hard races. In October 2017, Courtney won the Tahoe 240-mile race outright in 57 hours 55 minutes, beating second place (first male) by 10 hours. There's Jasmin Paris's dominant 2019 Spine Race victory; Samatha Amend's (now Hudson-Figuera) overall win at the 2022 Grand Union Canal Race, 145 miles between Birmingham and London in the UK; and Camille Herron's outright win at the 2022 Jackpot 100, which was also the US National Championship, by almost 30 minutes. And these performances aren't new. In 1989, US runner Ann Trason won the Sri Chinmoy USA 24-Hour National Championship outright, covering 143 miles and 139 metres and, in the process, beating one of the strongest male fields in the history of 24-hour racing. In 2002 and 2003 another American, Pam Reed, took the overall win at the infamous Badwater ultramarathon, running 135 miles through Death Valley. While not definitive, these performances at least open the door to conversations around males not necessarily being dominant in longer endurance challenges due to their inherent sex-based advantage.

While there are many vocal opponents of the idea that, when it comes to ultrarunning, female runners might one day close the gap with males, I remain open-minded. And I'm not the only one. Here are some of the reasons why.

Firstly, the practical considerations. There are far fewer women than men in ultrarunning, right through the ranks from first-timers to elites. So, if we're looking at elite runners, who might only toe the line in a couple of 100-mile+ distance races each year, the probability of a world-class female runner being on the start line is much lower than that of a world-class male runner. In road and track ultras, where the number of variables is relatively low, genetically lucky males might be expected to maintain their physiological advantage over females and other males. But the longer the race and the more variables there are – weather, sleep deprivation, fuelling and hydration, navigation, altitude, temperature extremes and so on – the more opportunity there is to develop a skill set that narrows the physiological gap. During the 2019 Spine Race, Jasmin Paris famously dropped male competitor Eugeni Roselló Solé after they'd been running together for many miles as she knew she was the better navigator. It doesn't matter how fast you're running if you're not going in the right direction.

In a recent report compiled by RunRepeat.com and the International Association of Ultrarunners (IAU), researchers explored the trends in ultrarunning over the past 23 years. After analysing 5,010,730 results from 15,451 ultrarunning events – the largest analysis ever done on the sport – they came up with some interesting findings. These included the observation that, based on this sample, female ultrarunners are faster than male ultrarunners at distances over 195 miles. As the researchers noted:

'The longer the distance the shorter the gender pace gap. In 5Ks men run 17.9% faster than women, at marathon distance the difference is just 11.1%, 100-mile races see the difference shrink to just 0.25%, and above 195 miles, women are actually 0.6% faster than men.'

This finding is particularly surprising given that participation rates drop dramatically for women as the distances get longer. At races of up to 80 kilometres (50 miles), women make up between 20 per cent and 50 per cent of entrants, depending on the race. Above that distance, this drops to just 16 per cent, reducing as the distance increases. In an online article, British ultrarunner Robbie Briton analysed competitor numbers from the 2018 UTMB races, finding a similar pattern, with female entrants comprising:

- 9.5 per cent at the 170-kilometre (106-mile) Ultra-Trail du Mont Blanc (UTMB)
- 11.4 per cent at the 119-kilometre (74-mile) Sur les Traces des Ducs de Savoie (TDS)
- 17 per cent at the 101-kilometre (63-mile) Courmayeur–Champex–Chamonix (CCC)
- 23.1 per cent at the 57-kilometre (35-mile) Orsières–Champex–Chamonix (OCC)

The RunRepeat report isn't the whole story, and neither does it promise to be. It's simply a gathering of past data, not a controlled research study. It doesn't separate results out into those held on the roads and track, where women might have more of a physiological disadvantage, and those held in open country where a far wider skill set can be brought to the race. And yet it does offer an interesting insight into the state of ultrarunning at a moment in time; and as simply as report of results – no more and no less – it provides some indication of what may be possible in the future.

Within ultrarunning, there are some who voice concern that women's participation in the sport would be negatively impacted if, in certain circumstances, the sex difference between female and male were to disappear. They fear that women's podiums might cease to exist; and that races and results could be presented as overall finish times and places, rather than by gender. I hope this is unlikely, as it would clearly be detrimental to both women's and men's ultrarunning; but I also think there's room to celebrate the intriguing puzzle of ultrarunning and the potential for women – and indeed everyone – to bring their unique skill set to the fore to reduce the gap created by pure physiological prowess. Women's races and women's results should absolutely be celebrated and protected for women, but is there not still some fun to be had – and huge strength and satisfaction to be taken – from being able to beat at least the vast majority of the boys?

Female runners may also have some interesting physiological advantages over males in longer races, especially those at altitude, according to research conducted by Dr Nick Tiller, an exercise scientist at Harbor-UCLA, columnist for *UltraRunning* magazine, writer and author. In his co-authored 2021 and 2022 papers, 'Do Sex Differences in Physiology Confer a Female Advantage in Ultra-Endurance Sport?' and 'Sex-specific Physiological Responses to Ultramarathon', he and a team of researchers investigated various physiological parameters in male and female time-matched runners at the 170k UTMB and how these changed over the course of the race.

The research found that female athletes exhibited numerous physiological traits that might confer an advantage in ultra-endurance challenges, including greater fatigue resistance, greater substrate efficiency and lower energy requirements. The negative effects of running an ultramarathon at altitude also appeared to happen less frequently and with a smaller effect size in female participants compared with males.

However, findings showed downsides of being female, too, including having a lower oxygen-carrying capacity, increased prevalence of GI distress and the potential effects of sex hormones on cellular function and injury risk.

The researchers highlight the small number of female participants in ultramarathons relative to males, meaning there's a far smaller field to choose from, whether you're conducting research or picking winners. It would also appear that the advantages of being female are most prominent over the longest distances, where currently the gap in participation is greatest. The article concludes:

'Crucially, the advantageous traits may only manifest

as ergogenic in the extreme endurance events which, paradoxically, are those that females less often contest.' It recommends that 'the title question should be revisited in the coming years, when/if the number of female participants increases.'

Nick kindly agrees to chat about his research and I ask him about the current gap between male and female performances.

'In running overall, depending on the research you're looking at, it's somewhere between 5 and 10 per cent,' he says. 'But if you look at long-distance swimming, females overall are faster than males, which is interesting. In long-distance cycling it's closer, too. But in running, it's the ultras that are closest.'

One of the things that excites me about ultras, and especially longer ultras in remote places, is that with such a small pace gap, optimizing everything else we do – nutrition and hydration, kit choice, navigation and self-care – can quickly make up for any inherent sex-based differences. I'm interested to know, from Nick's perspective, where he thinks women could focus their attention to exploit this potential.

'It's an important point that there are so many more variables in ultramarathon running than in other sports. In most other running distances, it's a physiological endeavour. If you think about a 1,500m race [almost a mile], about 75 per cent of performance can be predicted by VO_2max [oxygen uptake] – you have to have a high VO_2max. And it's very similar in marathon running – the best females will never beat the best males in marathon running because it's too heavily dependent on maximal aerobic capacities, and males just have bigger lungs and bigger cardiovascular systems. In ultra, not only is VO_2max less important – it's still a factor, it's still a predictive variable – but there are so many other things going on that it only takes a wrong kit choice; blisters, which wouldn't have so much of an effect over shorter distances, could easily make a 10 per cent difference; gastrointestinal distress and gut trainability; carbohydrate choice; whether your running pack is too tight, which over 100 miles might cause respiratory fatigue; how well you tolerate the heat; how much hill training you've done; whether you're using poles . . . There are all these different factors that mesh into this multifactorial predictive model, which I doubt will ever be possible to map out. It's just much more unpredictable. So that's an important point, that there are so many different things that can give you an advantage or a disadvantage in ultras, that it's feasible that one small decision can increase or decrease the gap.'

It's a similar story for increased age in ultrarunning, which confers both advantages and disadvantages for performance. Nick references a 2018 review paper by Beat Knechtle and Pantelis Nikolaidis, who looked at both the demographics of ultrarunning and the negative physiological effects the sport has on its participants.

The researchers found that as the duration of a race increased, so too did the age at which runners reached their peak performance. Over 6 hours, the mean age of peak performance was 34 years, rising to 44 years over 24 hours and 47 years over 48 hours. Harvey Lewis, record holder of the Backyard Ultra format of ultramarathon racing with 450 miles, was 47 when he set the record in 2023. Perhaps I really do have my best years still to come in ultrarunning.

Nick has some interesting thoughts around the potential impacts of increasing female participation in ultrarunning from the current 10–20 per cent average. It could, he suggests, increase the depth of the field and make females more competitive; or it could reduce the average time, making the average gap larger. Because one possibility is that the females who currently run ultras, and particularly the longer ultras, are self-selecting as the strongest and toughest, knowing they'll be competing against mostly males and taking into account the sociocultural aspects that go into that as well. So, it's possible that the females currently competing in ultra don't represent female runners more generally. We agree that the only way to answer this question is for more women to try ultrarunning.

Talking with Nick also gets me thinking about the other ways those without the physiological advantages of the fastest men can close the gap in events that require such a broad skill set to compete in. As I reflect on Jasmin Paris's achievements, it strikes me that her outstanding navigation skills and race strategy have also played a big part in her successes. Lacking confidence in navigation is an issue for many people, but in particular for women. It's nothing to do with how our brains work; but, like driving – especially in the past – from a sociocultural perspective it seems to more often be men who take the lead. Jasmin often talks about growing up hiking in the mountains with her family and going on multiday adventures with her brother. Navigation and self-management in remote environments are things she's simply always done. If we want to help more women achieve their dreams and their potential in ultramarathons, but also more generally in the world of outdoor adventure, it seems vital to equip all children with these basic skills.

Nick's great, a knowledgeable male ally for female runners, and his work is incredibly important. However, even though he's softly spoken and thoroughly considers every point before making it, how is it that the loudest voice in female ultrarunning physiology is a man's? I'm keen to talk to some women working in sport and exercise science, so I send out some emails to the women whose papers I've read and who I see presenting at conferences. But I get no replies. Nick's given me a few names to contact, but again I can't get in touch with them. Eventually, a physiologist replies, referring me to one of her male colleagues, who is, in her words, 'more of an expert in this area'. I ask a friend of mine who has a PhD in running biomechanics if she'd chat with me about the differences in the biomechanics of male and female runners. I know this friend would do anything to help, but she tells me she doesn't feel her expertise in this specific area is good enough. I think of the men who certainly shouldn't claim to be experts in running biomechanics but have nonetheless written books and given talks on everything from barefoot and forefoot running to the art of running that we humans have somehow 'lost'. How is it that they're happy to put themselves and their opinions out into the world when women who would be considered real experts in the subject shrink from the spotlight? When it comes to the gap between females and males, perhaps there are similarities between the worlds of sport and science.

* * *

Watching the 2020 documentary *Picture a Scientist*, it hits me like a wall. A wall that shouldn't be there. The statistics are stark: in the US, 50 per cent of undergraduate students in STEM (science, technology, engineering and maths) are women. As we move through masters, PhD and postdoctoral levels, this percentage gradually declines until we reach the workplace, where only 29 per cent of positions in STEM subjects are held by women. For black women, the percentage is even lower and showing some worrying trends. A 2023 report by the Education Trust suggests that the percentage of black women awarded PhDs in STEM subjects decreased from 1.3 per cent to 1.1 per cent between 2010 and 2019.

The mechanism by which women are lost from science-related fields over the course of their careers has been termed 'the leaky pipeline'. Women in science are, in the words of one male interviewee in the documentary, walking into a headwind that doesn't exist for men. Intentional and overt gender- and sex-based discrimination and sexual harassment are the tip of an iceberg. But beneath that iceberg lurk the far more difficult to quantify daily instances of implicit bias, whereby the unconscious decisions we all make, based on conditioning and association – in this case, the kinds of jobs and lives that we unconsciously associate with females and males – help to shape and determine the trajectory of people's lives.

I've worked in sports science for a long time, but, like so many others, have struggled to make it fit in terms both of the requirements of a life as a parent and simply feeling at home in a male-dominated field. My first attempt at a PhD ended after my daughter was born as trying to combine research and childcare just didn't feel possible. Completing a PhD then felt like something I'd failed at – a niggling, unfinished yet important project – so, a decade later, I decided to apply again. This time, I was interested in the more experiential side of running: I was fascinated by the lived experiences of distance runners rather than the biomechanical forces and pressures the sport involves. So, instead of looking at the location and frequency of running injuries, I wanted to know what being injured *meant* to runners – what running gave them and what injury took away. I applied for a few advertised PhDs, hoping to find one that worked for me as someone who needed to fit my studies around work, childcare and inability to drive. It felt like a long shot, but if I didn't try I'd never know.

I attended a number of interviews in which I wasn't successful. In one, I was even asked whether I was planning on having any more children. But eventually, I found my place, thanks to a female academic who believed I could complete a PhD despite personal circumstances far removed from those of a typical postgraduate student. It's an opportunity that has changed my life, and one I'm grateful for every day.

As I contact women in sport science now, I'm struck by something that feels fundamental. Women in areas of sport science where greater numbers of women are currently working – psychology, sociology, even philosophy – are more than happy to chat. Those in the more male-dominated fields – physiology, biomechanics – either don't reply or suggest I speak to a male colleague. I don't blame them in the slightest. On many occasions in the past, both in person and online, I've been talked over, edged out, even shouted down by a more numerous, more established group of men. My response has been to give up defending myself, or trying to make myself heard, and instead retreat to a place of safe anonymity, my head firmly below the parapet.

As I'm exploring the dynamics and disappearance of women from STEM subjects further, I spot an invitation to take part in a survey by Dr Emma Cowley, whose Invisible Sportswomen project aims to highlight the sex data gap in sport and exercise science research. Emma's 2021 paper, co-authored with three other women and published in the journal *Women in Sport and Physical Activity*, reviewed around 5,261 publications, with 12,511,386 participants included in the analyses. Overall, 63 per cent of publications included both males and females; but, while 31 per cent included only males, just 6 per cent included only females. An analysis of all the participants included found that 66 per cent were male, whereas only 34 per cent were female.

'The problem is,' Emma says, 'we know there are differences between males and females, but we don't know where and how – or even if – these differences should affect recommendations for health, training and performance. There might be a difference in an area, or there might not; and currently, because the data on females isn't there, we just don't know.'

As the paper indicates, because females remain significantly underrepresented within sport and exercise science research, there's a real danger that conclusions drawn from current research might be applicable to only one sex.

Emma's latest research explores the difficulties and barriers that exist for women in sport and exercise academia, and why so many women disappear from academia rather than progressing through the ranks as men do. The focus group I'm invited to participate in has been organized to discuss this phenomenon and we spend an hour sharing our experiences, from the assumption that women are expected to drop work commitments to provide childcare, whereas with men it's often the other way around, to having to adopt a more 'male' persona to be taken seriously.

I leave the meeting thinking it's far less about women and men than about the narratives and expectations we all carry around with us, that structure the worlds we inhabit and that so profoundly affect our own and others' experiences and opportunities. In a way, it's depressing, finding ourselves in a male-dominated world where everything from architecture to personal protective equipment is designed to suit men, and women can often feel at most like an afterthought. But this status quo exists because for decades it's been predominantly men – and predominantly white, educated, wealthy, able-bodied men – who have been out there creating it. For any inequity, change starts with noticing and acknowledging it exists. Then we can get on with making meaningful changes.

4

FINDING DIRECTION

'I think 100-milers are almost certainly a terrible idea
and when they involve mountains, they often involve
two nights without sleep, which is an even more
terrible idea. So, you should definitely do it.'
—Kirsty Reade, ultrarunning commissioning editor

t is the week of Ultra-Trail du Mont Blanc (UTMB) –
the race that's often considered the unofficial world
championships of ultra-trail running. Various races have
taken place over the previous days, from the Mini UTMB
kids' races to the 300-kilometre (186-mile) Petite Trotte à
Léon (PTL) for intrepid teams of three, and it is at last nearly
time for the start of the main event – the UTMB itself. In the
build-up to the race, I've watched the athletes do their pre-
race interviews, their bodies honed by thousands of hours
of running in the mountains, decked out in sponsored kit.
Each runner exudes an air of calm confidence, chatting with
the interviewers about their preparation, their race victories,
their strategy, knowing they've done everything possible to

this point. I feel like an obsessed teenager and find myself longing to be like them – to know the mountains and how to move my body through them as they do.

It's just before 6pm local time in the centre of Chamonix – a small town at the foot of Mont Blanc in the French Alps – and the main event of this supreme festival of ultra-trail running is about to begin. The UTMB covers around 171 kilometres (106 miles) of distance with around 10,000 metres (32,800 feet) of elevation gain. Competitors must complete the race in less than 46 hours and 30 minutes. 2022 sees 2,795 runners heading into the mountains from Chamonix, of which 9.3 per cent of starters, and 7.7 per cent of finishers, are women.

I watch them, taking it all in – the atmosphere, the excitement – wondering how it must feel to be on that start line. Stirring music builds – Vangelis's Conquest of Paradise – uniting the vast crowd as everyone strains to catch a glimpse of the runners. Camera flashes flicker across a sea of people. The picture zooms in on the competitors, colourful in running kit, caps, packs, poles, shoes designed for grip and precision on mountain terrain. Some look psyched-up, eyes wild, jumping on the spot; others are calm, collected and focused, waiting for it all to begin. The group jostles forward, the fastest runners taking their places at the front. And then they're off – streaming out of Chamonix's Place de l'Eglise, then on, up, into the mountains and into the first night.

I know, at this moment, that I must run my 100-mile race through the mountains. I know that this needs to be by far the hardest thing I have ever done – something that will terrify me and take me well beyond anything I have experienced before. That woman I found waiting for me as I emerged from early motherhood, the self I have recently been reunited with and seen afresh and anew, has spoken.

If you're going to do this, she said, *you're going to do it properly.*

It doesn't take long to find a race that even my fearless past self would have found daunting. Billed as the UK's first Alpine-scale ultramarathon, the Ultra-Trail Snowdonia (UTS) would be, according to its director, 'Beautiful beyond belief. Savage beyond reason.' Covering 165 kilometres (103 miles) and taking in 10,000 metres (32,800 feet) of ascent along the way, this is truly comparable to the ultramarathons held in the mountains of Europe and the US – only, with up to 48 hours of notorious Welsh weather thrown in. It would be a big ask even for those seasoned mountain runners whose names I know so well. With only six months to prepare and precious little access to the kind of terrain I would encounter at the race, it would surely be madness – wouldn't it?

Right then and there, before any hint of reason can cut through my overexcited impulsiveness, I sign up.

* * *

Through the bedroom window, in the early-morning gloom, I can make out the dark bulk of the mountains the moment I wake. Above them, Venus hangs huge and bright amid a scattering of faint stars. Within an hour, sunlight spills over the summits, liquid gold, honeying the rocky crags and gullies, running over the treeline, down alpine pastures grazed by lean brown cows that fill the hills with the music of their bells. Paling as it descends, the light ignites each chalet: those highest on the mountainside first, then eventually the valley below – the village with its church, school and shops, the people already going about their morning chores – filling the day with sunshine.

When we first arrived in these mountains, in the Beaufortain region of the Savoie en Rhône-Alpes in France, I had been entirely overawed by them. It took a day or two to become less daunted by the giants that surround us, to accept their presence without dreading it. Now, they still make my heart race but it is with excitement rather than fear. Every time I glimpse them – and it is hard to move more than a few steps from our rented apartment without doing so – I'm drawn to them. They have become an obsession, fed by daily visits to their high places, the punishment of their steepness, the rewards of their summits. They have entered every part of my being, filling my days and my nights.

We are here, among other reasons, to begin the long process of turning me from an efficient lowland runner, accustomed to running on flat towpaths and gently undulating trails, into a strong and agile mountain goat, capable of running for hours over steep, technical and precipitous terrain. I have read everything, watched everything and listened to everything I can lay my hands on to learn the theory of running in high places. Now, eye-to-eye with the mountains, I simply need to get out there.

Predictably, my first run in the mountains is a disaster. Terrified of everything in this unfamiliar setting, I've chosen an easy-to-navigate trail, linking up the hairpins on a steep road that winds its way up to a mountain pass at 1,700 metres (5,577 feet). As my starting point at the chalet is a little over 1,000 metres (3,280 feet), I've decided this will be a good introduction to running on higher, steeper ground, without too much objective danger.

Things start well and I zigzag my way up the mountainside, pleasantly surprised by my legs' willingness to cooperate with the climb, often finding myself running on the road between short sections of trail. Cars, motorbikes and road bikes crawl past me on their way up, whizzing by shortly afterwards on their way back down. Why, I wonder vaguely, through the stinging blur of sweat, aren't they spending longer up there? Beneath my feet I read names of Tour de France riders in colourful scrawl across the road, another group of athletes for whom regularly pushing the limits of physical and psychological exertion is entirely normal. I think of the peloton and its entourage squeezed onto this narrow road – where at times it feels like there's barely enough room for myself and a car to pass.

'*La route du barrage est fermée!*'

A man on an electric bike is calling out to me, waving to attract my attention. After a pause, he adds, 'Closed!' That I'm English, rather than a local trail runner, must be painfully obvious.

'*C'est loin?*' I call back, wanting to know how far I can go before having to turn around and simply run back down the same bit of road I've just come up.

'*Deux kilomètres,*' he replies, before disappearing down the next hairpin.

I feel frustration well up within me. This is what I get in return for the lack of imagination and/or courage that has me running up a road instead of exploring the hundreds of miles of waymarked trails that lead away to adventurous destinations in every direction. Even though it's not my fault that the road is closed, there's a certain pathetic inevitability about it. I think of Sim, who, on that first morning in the Alps, had run to the top of the Grand Mont, the highest mountain in the range at 2,686 metres (8,812 feet) and got back in time for lunch as if it was no big deal.

When I return to the chalet, after several failed attempts to find alternative routes to the top, or at least somewhere more exciting than the road, I've covered a grand total of 10 kilometres (6 miles), with 500 metres (1,640 feet) of vertical gain. It's not what I'd set out to do, but at least it's something – I've completed my first run in the mountains. As I enjoy the pleasant post-run achiness in my legs it hits me: I'll need to run ten times further, and climb twenty times higher, if I'm to finish Ultra-Trail Snowdonia.

I spend the night in a pit of negativity. What am I doing? Why on earth had I thought that signing up to run 100 miles through the mountains was in any way a good idea? Shouldn't I be taking care of my temperamental body, nurturing it with gentler activities instead of subjecting it to more trauma? Yet again, I think, I'm setting myself up for failure, taking on something that's so ridiculously beyond my capabilities it may as well be flying.

The next day, fuelled by the fire of the previous day's disappointment, things feel a little better. Ignoring the niggling voice of fear that whispers about the many dangers that might be waiting for me, I follow the dog along a tiny, winding, precipitously steep trail up through woodland and out onto open Alpine pasture and then on into the mountains. As I climb, views unfold all around me – a grand arena encircled by jagged peaks and scalloped slopes on every side, the vast bulk of the Mont Blanc massif in its bright white mantle towering over us all. Stopping to breathe, to allow my racing heart to slow just a little and my ears to adjust to the confusing absence of sound, I finally find what I've wanted for so long but that fear has so nearly deprived me of. Amid the nerves and exertion, the exposure and the grandeur, I begin to feel something like love.

* * *

In the apartment, high on a steep hillside beneath the mountains, our days revolve around a simple routine. We get up at six, make coffee and work until the children wake up. Then we have breakfast together and plan the day – school lessons and a walk or other adventure with the kids, and a run each.

The dog is beside himself, electric with excitement about being here. He is desperate to come on every run, every walk, every trip to a local lake, where he swims joyfully in the bright, clear water, propellor-tail wagging furiously as he goes. He is so hungry from all this activity that he doesn't seem to be able to eat enough. At mealtimes he circles the table like a ravenous shark with big, brown doggy eyes. The kids give in to his doleful gaze, feeding him pizza, omelette and toast from the table, something that would never be allowed at home. As well as his usual meals, he hoovers up leftover rice, pasta and cheese rinds, then asks for more. We begin to wonder whether we should limit the amount of exercise he does before we all run out of food. As we run more, Sim and I begin to experience something similar, constantly roving in search of calories to fuel the daily processes of running and repairing. In terms of becoming more accustomed to running in high, steep places, things are improving a little, but I'm still struggling to really get what I want from this trip.

We're a week into our time in the Alps when I find myself mid-rant at Sim. I've been vaguely aware that this has been building – a tension, an irritation, a niggle that I haven't quite been able to pin down. This afternoon, it fizzes to the surface and bubbles over. I tell him that I'm finding his machismo about his running conquests difficult. That here I am, struggling with even the most basic routes, when he seems to conquer a new mountain – or several new mountains – every time he goes out, returning with summit selfies, his handsome face grinning at the camera as if he's barely noticed the thousand metres he climbed to get there. I know he's hurting from his exertions, hobbling about after any big run; but these war wounds, it seems, just add to the glory.

By contrast, my efforts feel utterly pathetic. Fighting back pointless tears, I try to explain that it's not anything he's doing on purpose, or even anything he's even doing wrong, but I'm finding it hard not to wonder why on Earth I'm the one signed up to a ridiculous mountain race when he is clearly so much better at all this than I am. I admit that I feel disheartened when he comes in ravenous, muddied and bloodied yet triumphant after his epics, showing me the massive numbers for ascent and calorie expenditure on his watch. I rage on, listening to the dreadfulness of the words I am saying with growing irritation and detachment – as if another, more rational part of my brain cannot believe what it is hearing.

I imagine Sim can't believe it either. He asks me what he can do differently to help; tells me that he thinks I'm doing amazingly, seeing as this is something so new. All anger evaporates as I meet his gaze, finding something between concern and bemusement in those disarming blue eyes. Now I feel like a horrible wife as well as a crap runner.

Outburst over, I take my laptop outside to write. I gaze across the valley, breathe deeply into the mountain air and try to work out why I feel like this. Why can't I just be happy with my plan to build the amount of distance and ascent gradually as my body and mind adapt to these new conditions? Why do I find it so hard to accept that I'm not as good at this as I want to be, when all I need to do is give myself the time and opportunity to improve? I had planned a rest day for today, but this is making me feel scratchy and irritated, as if I'm wasting time by not running. My knees tell me otherwise, still aching from the previous day's punishment. I know what they need is rest.

Training for running or any athletic endeavour is always a balancing act. It is the art of applying enough damage to stimulate adaptation but not so much as to cause injury. It is also about managing the mind, balancing the motivation to push hard with the discipline to be patient. I know I crave the peace and satisfaction that come from having completed a hard run, but today I must wait. If I stick to my plan, I'll reap the rewards tomorrow, when I can conquer my own, smaller summits with fresh legs and renewed determination.

I soon realize that rest days are a real problem for me. These periods of relative stillness, in such stark contrast to the adrenaline buzz and hard physical labour of the mountains, torment my mind, even if I know beyond any doubt that I need them. I think it is a combination of fatigue from running, an inexplicable inability to sleep well most nights and anxiety about my next run. Before a run, my mind fills with worries about what might happen to me out there. During a run, I exist in a state of heightened awareness, ready for anything – cliff edges, savage dogs, lone men, all of which I meet at various times and none of which prove to be a problem. Rest days are stressful for their lack of running. It's only in the brief moments immediately after running that I feel soothed and at peace – only then do I know I have conquered both myself and the mountain; that I was brave and strong enough; and that I am still alive. Only then is the beast quiet – for a short time, at least.

* * *

During our stay in the Alps I'm keen to visit Chamonix, a mecca for all things mountain ultrarunning and home to the UTMB. We get there early on a Sunday morning and walk through the quiet streets, enjoying having this usually busy place to ourselves for a while.

'Mummy, are you cold?' Hugo, feeling my hand shaking as he holds it tightly in his, looks up at me in concern. I try to explain to him that no, I'm not cold, I'm just . . . I search for the word, barely understanding what the sensation is myself. Is it . . . *buzzing*?

I've only ever seen this place while watching the annual footage of the UTMB. It therefore feels a little like I'm walking through the set of one of my very favourite films. It's how I imagine someone who loves football must feel on their first visit to Wembley. Though the streets are quiet now, it's as if the echoes of the drama that unfolded here only a month ago – the music, the cheers of the crowd, the painful successes and failures of the runners – all still hang, tantalizingly, in the air.

As we wander these oddly familiar streets, sports shops and cafes are busy welcoming the first visitors of the day. The kids press their noses against a patisserie window, marvelling at piles of colourful macarons. We stand for a while, watching the great bells swinging in the Benedictine tower of St Michel's, ringing out into the hills, into the spires and turrets of the Mont Blanc massif that towers above us all. Mont Blanc herself is resplendent, dazzlingly white as the morning sun reaches her upper slopes, soft curves majestic and composed above the jagged pinnacles of the Aiguilles (or 'needles'). The UTMB course circumnavigates this great mountain – the highest in Europe – and I can't imagine a better way to pay one's respects.

There are some in the mountain-running world who complain that UTMB is becoming too big, too commercial. A restructure in 2022 saw the brand join up with Ironman and expand globally. Now, races across the world bear the 'by UTMB' branding, indicating that they are events at which runners can gain qualification points – or 'stones' – that allow them to apply for the UTMB itself. Critics suggest this could encourage unsustainable levels of travel as runners tick off bucket lists of UTMB races.

It's a complex case, a brand capitalizing on the rapid growth of a fairly niche sport; but the UTMB brand is also responsible for this growth, for bringing the drama and excitement of running long distances through the mountains to a wider audience. Arguably, having more 'by UTMB' races available for those who want to participate in the grand finale in Chamonix each year means less need for travel, as more people will have access to a nearby event. And for those who prefer a smaller, more intimate racing experience with fewer competitors, lower entry fees and no grand start or finish line, the sport is expanding everywhere – there's plenty of choice for everyone.

* * *

Over the month we spend in the Alps, I feel the mountains beginning to change what I believe is possible. My runs gradually get longer, higher, more adventurous. I still spend the night before each one sleepless and fearful, and the runs themselves in a state of jumpy hyper-alertness; but despite all this I notice I can take on just a little more each time, feeling slightly less overawed by the combination of solitude, altitude and general, anxiety-inducing unfamiliarity.

Still, some runs don't go to plan. One morning I climb over 600 metres (1,969 feet) at the start of a loop I've planned to run – a route recommended by Sim, who ran it the previous day. Approaching the top, I'm met with a massive explosion just a little way ahead. The sound ricochets around the mountains, a terrifying booming that fills the space in every direction. I stop, ears ringing, heart racing, brain struggling to comprehend what the hell is going on. I stand shaking, gasping with fear and altitude, trying to take in this new horror. Once the echoes have faded, I decide to wait for a few minutes to let my heart rate slow and to try to work out what to do next. But another explosion sends me scurrying straight back down the way I came, with no thoughts other than getting back to the safety of the valley, away from the fearful mountains and their dreadful noises.

It later turns out that it wasn't explosions that sent me careering off the mountain, but gunshots, courtesy of *la chasse* – hunting season. In the Alps, this tradition sees predominantly grandfathers, fathers and sons head into the mountains on select days each week between September and February to shoot the local populations of marmots, ibex, mouflon, wild boar and chamois. It's tolerated because it's traditional; because it's for the men; because, unlike hunting in the UK, it isn't elitist and doesn't prevent the public accessing large swathes of wild land; and because it helps with the need to cull overpopulating species locally. *La chasse* is therefore part of French rural life. Unfortunately, permitted hunting days always include weekends and public holidays, so they also coincide with the times French kids, and those adults who enjoy other leisure activities, are free to roam safely in the great outdoors. Many hunting-related accidents happen each year, mostly involving the hunters themselves but also folk out enjoying the countryside. Consequently, there are around 120 fatalities annually.

Many younger French people and those referred to as 'women's groups' are campaigning to have hunting banned on Sundays; but as I write this, in a time when every vote counts for marginal governments in polarized countries across the world, it isn't looking likely. The advice for those venturing out on hunting days is to wear bright colours, keep to well-used tracks and look out for signs warning that hunting is in progress: *Chasse en cours*. I hadn't seen one of these signs on my run, and must have been pretty close to the hunt, given how loud the gunshot was, so I decide to schedule my runs for non-hunting days as much as possible.

* * *

A few days before we leave the Alps, I plan a big last run – a celebration of the progress I feel I've made over the month we've been here. We need to take the dog to the vet in the nearby town of Albertville for the medication and health check necessary for him to return to the UK. Albertville is 30 minutes by car but looking at the map it's a little over 20 kilometres (12 miles) to run there straight from the chalet over the mountains, on what looks like good trails. I calculate that it should take me around 4 hours, given the terrain and ascent of around 1,000 metres (3,281 feet). Perfect.

I arrange with Sim to meet him at a park in the centre of the town, leave myself 5 hours to be on the safe side – as the main French speaker, I don't want to miss the vet appointment. Then I pack my running vest with food, water and emergency kit and head off up the first climb into the mountains.

I love maps, and they're invaluable when it comes to planning adventures, but one thing maps can never do is tell you what it will feel like to be out there in the middle of it all. They don't tell you about the burning sun, the dry air, the effects of altitude, the scary dog that will run at you barking furiously, the exhilaration of making it to your highest point yet, or that you won't see a single other person all day long. Maps won't suggest packing spikes for the still-deep snow lying in some of the higher, north-facing gullies, or that you'll need to fold up your poles so you can use your hands to balance along a knife-edge ridge. Maps are entirely devoid of context. They won't tell you which stretches of the red dotted line that delineates a path will fill you with pure joy at being alive, or which sections will make you question your own limits when it comes to risk.

By the time I reach the rocky climb to the final summit before the final descent to Albertville, I have experienced all these things and much more. I can see the cross on the last top. The map shows an easy line down the mountain. I think of the anxiety that had filled me before leaving – the thoughts of all that might go wrong out here – and feel relief that I've pretty much made it. I pick my way carefully up the path, which gradually becomes rockier and less distinct. I had assumed the path would lead me all the way to the final summit, but suddenly it ends abruptly: a sheer cliff dropping to a deep col between this first, false summit and the next – the true summit. I can't climb straight down, so I try traversing first around one side and then the other. In the end I give up – there seems to be no way across. The map shows a good path that leads around the base of this outcrop and then up to the summit. It's a long way down and back up again, but looks far safer and easier to navigate. I turn around and make my way back to a path junction I crossed half an hour ago, heading left this time and descending a few hundred metres into the valley below. Then, finding the right trail, I power hike my way back up again, regaining all my lost height, eventually arriving just below the main summit – the point I could see from my previous perch high on the rocky outcrop that led to nowhere. Now it's just a short traverse on that narrow path and I'll be at the summit.

But the route foils me yet again. A narrow, rocky ridge spans the distance between me and the final top. I can see no clear path, but the only possible way traverses below the ridge, crossing a steep scree slope that plummets hundreds of metres into the depths of the valley far below. I tell myself it is fine – this must be the way – talking out loud to calm my nerves. I fold up my poles; I'll need both of my hands to hold onto the ridge as I make the traverse. Then, after a deep breath, I edge out over the void, feeling its deadly pull beneath my feet.

I make it across the first section and then stop at a small ledge – the first solid ground I've found. I look back the way I've come, then ahead at the next section. I know I could reverse my steps to my starting point from here, but if I carry on . . . I'm not so sure. I think of the infamous Hinterstoisser Traverse on the north face of the Eiger and the chilling tale of those who made the first ascent, as described in Heinrich Harmer's legendary book *The White Spider*. That was the first book about climbing I ever read – I still recall the moment I spotted it on the shelves of our local library, aged about 11, and the utter absorbed fascination I felt on reading it. But the book comes with a lesson, learned by those who lost their team-mates on that ascent. When you're climbing into the unknown, never make any moves you can't reverse.

I bail. Again. Retreating across the scree slope until I can throw myself gratefully onto the solid ground I'd so unwillingly left behind me not long before. I feel tears of frustration welling up – why is this all so bloody hard? Why can't it just go to plan? I look at my watch – there's now no way I'm going to make it to Albertville in time to meet Sim and the kids before the vet appointment. I look at the map to see if there's any way to sort this ridiculous situation out without having to retrace my steps all the way back to our apartment. Eventually, I spot a trail that will take me down the side of the mountain to the valley and the tiny village of Queige over a thousand metres below. Luckily, I have phone signal. I ring Sim and explain apologetically that I'm not going to make it, that he's going to have to muster the required French to sort out the dog. He sounds slightly disbelieving, as I'd left myself so much extra time, but there's not much else he can do. We arrange to meet in Queige at some point, after the dog's appointment and after I've made my way off this mountain. When we've hung up, I send him a message with the French he's likely to need. Then I begin my descent to the valley.

It's a long, long way down. I ran out of water on the summit and, hours later, it's all I can think about. My mouth is so dry it sticks together and I fantasize about water. My route down traces the course of a river – gushing and tumbling with fresh, cold mountain meltwater – and I long with every parched cell of my body to dive in and drink it all. But it's far too dangerous to try to reach it. When I eventually find Sim and the kids, I can't even speak. I drain all the water they have with them and then, still thirsty, feel bad for doing so.

I look up at the final summit – the one that defeated me – and feel a mixture of emotions. In a way, I'd got everything I wanted out of this last Alpine run – a big adventure, lots of mountains, self-reliance, not dying. But I'm still frustrated that I didn't manage to make it to Albertville on time.

Risk is something I've been struggling with since deciding to learn to run in the mountains. As a parent, I'm not just taking risks for myself, but for my children. If I make a bad decision and don't come back, they grow up without a mother. It's a big deal.

Talking with other ultrarunning women helps me to see things more clearly. There is objective risk involved in being in mountainous places, of course, but probably not as much as my anxious mind tells me there is. The process I'm going through of slowly becoming accustomed to mountain environments will help me to feel more comfortable, a position from which I can make better decisions. Pre-kids, I spent a lot of time climbing, sometimes in the mountains, and got used to the sense of remote exposure typical of a hanging belay halfway up a vast rockface. I'd got good at supressing rising feelings of panic, and could still do that today if I found myself in a difficult place. But it's the anxiety of the night before a big mountain run that I'm finding so hard; the grumpiness, the stress. How can I be sure I'm not running to my death?

Jasmin Paris tells me there are times when she questions whether the risks she's taking are reasonable. She and her husband Konrad used to ski mountaineer, but she now chooses not to as the risks are too high. It's clear that Jasmin is nonetheless very much at home in mountain environments. As is Lake District-based Sabrina Verjee, who's triumphed in many epic mountain challenges – including claiming the record for the fastest continuous run of all 214 Wainwrights (Lakeland fells, all but one of which are over 305 metres/1,000 feet), a distance of 523 kilometres (325 miles), and winning the Tor des Géants (TOR 330) – a 330-kilometre (205-mile) race in Italy's Aosta Valley. 'I feel far safer in the mountains than in the city,' Sabrina tells me. 'I'd much rather run through the fells at night than Manchester.'

Assessing risk, whether we're in the mountains or the city, is something we all do. But personal safety is something women in particular learn to fear for from an early age. A 2023 survey of 9,000 runners undertaken by Adidas found that 92 per cent of women fear for their safety while running. Half of those surveyed were afraid of being physically attacked, and over a third had experienced physical or verbal harassment. Of these women, over half had received unwanted attention, sexist comments or unwanted sexual attention, been honked at, or followed.

It's something I talk to Sim about, discussing our differing levels of anxiety when it comes to running. Before a run, he considers the basic practicalities – things like shoes, clothing, food, water, safety (in case he comes across someone else who needs help, he hastens to add) and navigation. I consider all these things, but also the safety of my route for me as a lone woman. He has no fear about anyone he meets out running, whereas I'm constantly on alert, constantly assessing situations, knowing that while the likelihood of being raped and murdered is incredibly small, it's far more likely to happen to a woman than a man. Sport psychologist Dr Carla Meijen sums it up – 'There's no such thing as a "male" or "female" brain,' she tells me. 'But the experience of a run, the perception of safety, is totally different for men and women.'

Over 25 years of running, I've experienced a few worrying incidents. Not many were serious, but all left me feeling violated in some way and two were genuinely frightening. The first of these happened in my late 20s, when I was running home from the gym at about 7pm – something I did a few times each week. As I ran down a footpath, two men appeared and tried to grab me. Instinctively I sped up and managed to get free, but got spat at as I left them behind. On the second occasion, I was in my late 30s or early 40s and running with the dog. On a quiet section of towpath, a man simply stood in my way and wouldn't let me pass, preferring to stand and shout misogynistic insults at me. The dog put himself between me and the man, barking furiously, which eventually put him off – but not before he'd swung unwisely in the dog's direction. I called the police both times and both times was treated with absolute respect and care. The list of minor incidents – shouting, lewd comments, honking and so on – is too lengthy to put here. But, in short, it's definitely a problem.

As for being more comfortable running in the mountains, I decide I just need to allow myself more time. For the most part, the women I speak to about risk look at me like I'm asking a slightly ridiculous question. Why choose to run and race in the mountains if it scares me so much when there are plenty of flat 100-milers to choose from? And, of course, this is the very reason I want to learn to run in the mountains – for the thrill and exhilaration that comes from being in high, wild places. I think my mind just needs time to acclimatize, in the same way my body does when I'm running in the Alps at higher altitude.

5

JOINING THE DOTS

'In an ultramarathon you come face-to-face with yourself at your most naked. And ultimately, it's your choice – you choose to continue or you choose to stop. You're constantly asking yourself: why am I here? It's got to be more than a time or a t-shirt – it's got to be an inner feeling of knowing this journey is part of a bigger journey.'

—Sabrina Pace-Humphreys, author of *Black Sheep*, co-founder of Black Trail Runners

As each runner in Big's Backyard Ultra fails to complete their last loop, or fails to start the next one, Gary Cantrell, also known as Lazarus 'Laz' Lake, hands them a scrap of paper with the following message handwritten on it: 'You can't accomplish anything without the possibility of failure.' It's simultaneously an acknowledgement that they've taken on something huge and scary, that they're awesome for doing so, and a damning indictment of their inability to achieve the sole

THE PATH WE RUN

goal of backyard ultras: to be the last person standing. For in backyard ultrarunning, there is, at the most, only one winner. Everyone else fails – the dreaded DNF.

Backyard ultras were Laz's idea – he's well known for organizing races that blend immensely difficult physical and psychological challenges. But, due to the simple genius of the concept, it has spread globally. The format is deceptively straightforward: a 6.7-kilometre (4.167-mile) loop that runners must complete once an hour, starting on the hour. As the original Big's race looped the Tennessee backyard patrolled by Cantrell's dog, Big, each loop is known as a 'yard'. Runners who complete 24 yards have therefore run 100 miles in 24 hours.

From its conception in 2011, when Tim Englund – a maths teacher from Washington – completed 18 yards, the backyard-ultra record has been steadily extended. Englund won again in 2013 with 35 yards. In 2019, US ultrarunner Maggie Guterl became the first female overall winner, running 60 yards (402.4 kilometres/250.02 miles). The following year, Courtney Dauwalter (a former high-school science teacher) raised the record to 68 yards, beating compatriot Harvey Lewis (also a teacher) who dropped out at 67. Lewis set a new record of 108 yards (724 kilometres/ 450 miles) in 2023, beating Ukrainian-Canadian Ihor Verys to be the last man standing. In a 2023 article in The *Guardian,* while discussing the late stages of that race, Laz observes: 'It's a quandary, because Ihor is clearly the stronger runner, but Harvey won't give up. And you don't have to be the strongest runner. You just have to be strong enough.'[1]

It's a great example of the power of the mind in ultrarunning. And how much mental toughness you need to be a teacher.

One of the most intriguing things about backyard ultras – and a nod to Laz's genius when it comes to creating races – is that a minimum of two runners is required for the race to continue. The winner is the last person standing, the moment they complete the last loop that no one else completed within the allowed hour. So, who knows how far Maggie or Courtney could have run in either of their winning years if they'd had an 'assist' (Laz's word for the second-to-last person standing) who'd been able to carry on?

For many – me included – the fear of failure is strong. Sometimes, I think I'd rather not try something than give it everything and fail. Failure hurts. It brings with it shame, embarrassment, vulnerability. But, as Laz points out in his post-backyard message, it's also an inevitable part of doing hard things – and a risk whenever we take on something that's truly challenging.

I've failed at lots of things in the past and sometimes the sting hasn't faded. But failures have also been some of my

---

1 Palmer, J. (2023) 'Ultrarunner Harvey Lewis reaches the end of Lazarus Lake's endless backyard', *The Guardian*. Available at: https://www. theguardian.com/sport/2023/oct/27/harvey-lewis-ultramarathon-backyard-championship (Accessed: 07 June 2024).

most important learning experiences. Success can bring complacency, but failure brings fire.

Another of Laz's races, another intricate intermingling of physical and psychological challenge and another place where failure is almost always the only option, is the notorious Barkley Marathons. Shrouded in myth and secrecy, the event is held in Frozen Head State Park in Tennessee every year, usually in late March, and, at the time of writing, has seen only 20 finishers in its 38-year history.

Runners who wish to take part must go through an application process that includes writing an essay and paying a $1.60 registration fee. Successful applicants receive a letter of condolence, informing them they have secured a place in the event. First-timers are required to bring a car license plate from their home country, while returning runners who failed their previous attempt must bring a specified item – in the past this has included a shirt or socks. For returning finishers, it's a packet of Camel Cigarettes. The race itself is billed as 100 miles – competitors run 5 circuits of a 32-kilometre (20-mile) loop around the steep, briar-filled woods of the park, much of which is out of bounds to the public at any other time – but many speculate it's much further. It's a self-navigated challenge with a 60-hour cutoff and no GPS or even distance data allowed – each runner is provided with a simple watch showing only the race time. Each lap, runners are required to locate between 9 and 14 books that are hidden in the woods and retrieve the page that corresponds to their race number, which changes for each loop. The loops start and finish from the famous yellow gate at Frozen Head public campground, where runners have a tent or vehicle, supplies and support that they return to in between each loop (known at Barkley as the interloopal period).

Whether a woman can finish Barkley has long been a question within ultrarunning circles – a question that remained unanswered until 2024. Laz, famous for making controversial statements designed to get exactly this kind of debate going, had stated that he believed it would never happen. In a brilliant blog post in 2018, Tennessee-based data scientist John Kelly – an incredibly talented endurance athlete, father of four and already two-time finisher when the 2024 race began – argued that it was perfectly possible. It was just a matter of the right woman turning up and having enough luck with the elements out of any runner's control (weather, injury and so on) to do so.

At 21:17 on 22 March 2024, those who had been following the final moments of the Barkley Marathons breathed a collective sigh of relief. The news broke that Jasmin Paris had finished the fifth and final loop in a time of 59:58:21 – just 99 seconds inside the cutoff time. The footage of Jasmin running down the finishing strait, her sole focus the yellow gate at the far end, and promptly collapsing when she got there has been shared widely, including on BBC News, which also aired an interview with her a couple of days later. It's an incredibly emotional video, summing up exactly what it had taken to be the first woman to finish the

Barkley: in a word, everything. But in giving it everything – it was Jasmin's third attempt at the race, having attempted it in 2022 and 2023 – she had proved it was possible for a woman to finish.

Now aged 40, Jasmin had brought exactly the combination of physical and psychological ability, experience, self-management, navigation, kit and luck (she managed to avoid illness and injury and had kind weather at Frozen Head State Park) required to even have a shot at a Barkley finish. Her name even begins with a J, a fact that makes her statistically significantly more likely to finish the race – which neatly demonstrates some of the limitations of statistics.

John Kelly also finished the 2024 race, becoming only the third person to have done so three times. As he later summed it up in an Instagram post accompanying a photo of the five successful finishers : 'Jasmin had all the right ingredients – incredible strength and speed, an unstoppable quiet resolve, master navigation, and amazing support from her husband Konrad. She failed in 2022 and 2023, but nevertheless, she persisted & gained valuable experience.'

As when Jasmin took her incredible overall victory on the Pennine Way in 2019, suddenly the eyes of the world were on this quietly spoken vet and academic from Scotland and an obscure race that represented an extreme test of human endurance. In an emotional interview, she dedicated her finish to women, saying: 'Whatever adventure you have, you need to believe in yourself – to be willing to take some risks and give it a go. I came back three times – I believed it was possible. It's worth putting the effort in if there's something you really want.'

John Kelly was at the finish with his young family, waiting to congratulate Jasmin as she proved his theory right. The final line of his post celebrates the true meaning of the achievement:

'My daughters were there watching. Thank you Jasmin, for showing them what I never fully could.'

* * *

It's October, and more than a year until Jasmin will make her historic Barkley finish. With seven months to go until my own 100-mile adventure, I'm searching for clues. What can I do today and during each day, week and month between now and then that will bring me a step closer to being brave enough to start this race and sufficiently prepared to finish it? In some respects, it feels like I'm still a long way from that start line. But I've met – and missed – enough deadlines to know that the time will pass in a flurry of everything I need to do besides running.

One of the main reasons I want to take on this challenge is for representation. I see so few women, especially lone women, and even more especially older lone women running in mountainous places. And yet so many of the women I speak to only discovered their hidden endurance superpowers later on in life. I long to rewrite the narrative of decline that we are so often fed as we age; to prove that, as we disappear from certain areas of society, we can reappear on the trails, in the hills, in the mountains, living our best lives regardless of expectation.

This is all very well if I have a good race: if I fight hard, cross the finish line, and have at least some positive experiences to share. But if I don't do all these things – if I fail to fight, fail to finish or, even worse, fail to even start – then what message am I sharing? That we shouldn't be taking on these challenges? That's the last thing I want to say.

As I talk to more women about their experiences of ultrarunning, I realize the profound effect their stories are having on me – in how I approach my own running and how I view women's running and sport in a wider context. All of them showed up at their first race, their first ultra, their first 100-miler, unsure if it was something they could do. But showing up was the gutsy bit – that's when the fear and doubt and anxiety feel the worst. Once the gun goes off, it's hard to worry about much other than what's directly ahead. I feel a building wave of support for my own challenge as I share my hopes and fears with others and in turn hear theirs. As someone who's naturally shy in social situations, I've often lived on the edges, often held back from joining or joining in. My quest to discover what it takes to run 100 miles, though, is bringing me closer to the community of ultrarunning women. This community is a place of support and reassurance, where, because of the hardships we willingly put ourselves in the way of, even those competing against each other look out for each other.

Running has always been a way I can connect. Over the years, wherever I've lived, running has been a ready-made space where I feel I belong. I've forged friendships with those I've met through running that have lasted decades and I hope will last decades more. My regular running friends have become a particularly special part of my life. We all juggle running with our families and our jobs, and because of this we share an unspoken understanding. Sometimes we need to cancel at the last minute without being thought of as unreliable. Sometimes we need to run in comfortable, mutually understood silence. Sometimes we need to talk nonstop, venting or enthusing about something that's ongoing in life. We're all different, and the specifics of our lives are individual, but we're all navigating a similar stage in life – our children finding their way into double figures; the looming, but as yet mostly unknown, challenges of the menopause; health; love; relationships; work . . . These are women I know I can lean on, and I trust they know they can always lean on me. Even when we begin our early morning runs tired and tense, we always finish them feeling better.

It's unknown whether having children or not having children has any bearing on our ability to run ultramarathons, but it clearly affects our daily experiences of running, and for females far more than males. Pregnancy and birth change bodies. Abdominal muscles may not meet in the middle. Asymmetry and imbalance are common. The first years are a massive change to the normal structure of life for everyone involved and, for females, the process of having kids leaves lifelong marks on and in our bodies.

Most of us reach our endurance peak in our 30s, which is also when the vast majority of those who have children have children. From rehabilitation and return to running after giving birth to the years of juggling training and racing around the demands of being a parent, it seems logical that it would be impossible for childbearing to have no effect on our running.

'It always frustrates me that women are asked how they manage to fit running around their children, whereas no one ever asks men that question. When a woman with children wins a race, the headline is always, "Mum of three wins race", or even, "Super gran completes challenge"; but when a man wins you never read headlines saying, "Father of three wins race". It shouldn't be relevant either way.'

I'm chatting with sports historian Katie Holmes, who specializes in the history of women's running. I've followed her work for a long time, enjoying the snippets she unearths from history and shares with others and the insightful interviews, blog recommendations and especially the articles on older women in ultrarunning.

I completely agree with Katie. It's something I've also noticed and grumbled about often. But based on my own experiences, knowing just how much my running was changed by having kids, I'm not sure ignoring the issue is the way forward. When I speak with ultrarunner, coach and mum of three Eddie Sutton, who has finished on the podium in some of the toughest races around, including the Winter Spine race and the Northern Traverse, she shares similar experiences to my own when her children were small. 'In any long race, mentally – and physically – you break yourself down,' she says. 'And I found when I first had kids and they were little, I didn't have that mental strength to put myself in that hole, which I do have now. Often, I'd either stop or just have a terrible guilt-fest during ultras or training thinking I should be doing this, especially when I was still breastfeeding. But once they get older there's much less mum guilt, and you find you can actually push yourself harder because they're watching you. In the Spine Race, knowing the kids were at home watching my dot, and knowing if I didn't finish, I'd have to go home and explain why mummy quit to them really helped me keep moving forward.

'When you've had kids you're a different person: your body is different, the way you react to training is different, your times might be different. And for me, early on, that resulted in a lot of negative chatter in my head, saying how much slower I was, how tired I was, how everyone was going to be judging me – a lot of negative self-talk that I didn't have before. It took me a while to learn to listen to that and just say "thanks so much, but none of that is helpful to what I'm trying to do right now" and to change it into a positive – so I'm out here, I've done the training, okay, I might not be as fast as I used to be but I can still do these hard things. Nowadays, enjoying the process and simply finishing means much more to me than being on the podium.'

Eddie pauses and considers that for a moment. 'Actually, that's a lie because all I want to do is be on the podium! But now the kids are older I really think I'm stronger than I was. I don't think I could have done the Spine pre-kids – I really don't. I think I'd have stopped because it was so hard and because of what it was doing to my body. Having kids has made me mentally much stronger, but also more patient, and more able to focus my time for training. And even more so, now I'm a role model for my kids, especially for my little girl – I want her to know that she's just as capable of doing these things – if not more so – than her brothers.' After my conversations with both Katie and Eddie, I wonder whether instead of stopping asking women how they fit their running around their children, we should make sure we ask fathers and other non-childbearing parents the same question. So many of those whose epic running achievements we celebrate wouldn't be able to do any of it without a partner – usually a woman – looking after their children. And yet hardly ever are these partners recognized, championed, credited with their essential part in the story. Instead of pretending primary caregivers don't exist, shouldn't we demand their recognition?

Globally, women undertake three-quarters of unpaid work, predominantly caring, cooking and cleaning, with little recognition of its value. A recent report by Oxfam suggests that if we valued care work the same as traditional paid work, it would be worth nearly US $11 trillion (almost £9 trillion) a year.

But the narrative and, for many caregivers, the reality, are changing. The COVID-19 pandemic, for all its negatives, enabled more people to work flexible hours and from home, which makes a full working life more possible for those with caring responsibilities. Perhaps these changes have also allowed some of those who usually work away from home to more fully engage with family life, to feel a valued and integral part of the puzzle. Within ultrarunning specifically, it's refreshing to hear high profile male athletes like Kilian Jornet, John Kelly and Dylan Bowman sharing their experiences of becoming and being fathers, the juggle of fitting training and racing around family commitments, and acknowledging the importance of teamwork, allowing both parties to fulfil parental, career and athletic ambitions to whatever level they wish. As with so many other areas where inequity is rife, these are vitally important conversations with the potential to change things for the better for everyone involved.

* * *

One theme that shines through from my conversations with elite female ultrarunners is the importance of a strong support network. So many ultrarunning greats acknowledge the support of partners, parents, coaches and friends as foundational to their success. For mothers, having supportive partners and parents appears to be key – Jasmin Paris, for example, was able to be crewed by her husband, Konrad, at the Barkley Marathons because her parents were able to take care of the children.

Another theme is upbringing. Many ultrarunners talk about growing up with the support and encouragement to participate in activities such as running, hiking, climbing and skiing, learning to read a map, carry a rucksack and feel comfortable in wild places from an early age. A person's upbringing, though, is not something that's ever within their control. Role models – whether that's our parents, teachers or people in the public eye – are so important, because seeing the achievements of people we perceive as being sufficiently like us means we can imagine doing what they're doing. Our dreams can be inspired by theirs.

Certainly, there are many individuals – and many more women – in the world who could be outstanding ultramarathon runners if only particular things in their lives had been different. In reality, what makes a great ultrarunner, and especially one who can perform in events such as Barkley, is an intricate, lifelong accumulation of experience and the interaction of many different influences – far more than for those competing over shorter distances. It's a culmination of physicality, psychology, biomechanics, lifestyle, support, financial stability, luck . . . the list goes on. The stuff – the mental and physical prowess – of great ultrarunners and elite athletes is complex and multifaceted. While those who achieve incredible sporting feats can offer motivation and inspiration, we all have our own, unique, unchangeable history that shapes who we are today and, to a large extent, who and what we can become. Inspiration is helpful, but comparison isn't – something that, in a world where it's easy to feel we're never good enough, it's important to remember.

6

CHANGING THE NARRATIVE

'It takes a really long time to train for something like
this, to reach your potential. I think a lot of people
don't realise but it took me 10 years to reach a peak.
It's a really long journey, so you have to stick with it,
enjoy the process, and navigate the ups and downs
along the way.'

—Beth Pascall, Western States winner and
Bob Graham Round record holder

Sim and I have our birthdays either side of Christmas,
so we decide to spend a week in Eryri (Snowdonia)
with the excuse that it's a joint Christmas and
birthday present to each other. We find a cottage on Airbnb
with mountains on the doorstep that's just about within our
budget. It's perfectly placed, but tiny. That doesn't matter,
though: we'll sleep on camp beds downstairs while the kids
have the two beds upstairs. Apparently it has an enormous
bath, which I'd swap for a bedroom any day.

This will be my first trip to the area since entering UTS;

and, while I climbed here a bit during days long past, I haven't done much running in these mountains. The running I have done here was special, though. On one of our very first dates, Sim and I ran up Cadair Idris in the south of the National Park, climbing Whaleback Buttress alpine-style as we went. At the top, battling against the wind, we'd hurried into the stone shelter, grateful to be able to stand upright and hear each other again. As we sat sharing sweets, we chatted with an older couple who were happily enjoying a Sunday roast as if it were the most normal thing in the world.

On the way back down, I caught my shin on a sharp spike of rock, making a hole that oozed dark-red blood down my leg and into my sock. Partly because I didn't want to make a fuss to my beautiful new boyfriend, and partly because I was having too much fun, I ignored it and carried on, but it looked quite spectacular by the time we arrived back at the car. I still have the scar today – a nice reminder of those heady, hedonistic times we spent running, drinking wine and falling in love.

Eryri was also where I ran my first marathon – the Snowdonia Marathon (known as Marathon Eryri since 2023). I remember flying around the undulating, mostly tarmac route until the final few miles, where it left the roads and followed the Slate Trail steeply up from Waunfawr and then steeply back down again to finish in Llanberis. The moment the angle steepened and I began to climb, cramp gripped both sets of quadriceps, forcibly straightening both of my legs. I must have looked comical attempting to get up the hill without bending my knees. Despite the pain, the race has a place in my heart, and I still have the slate finishers' coaster on my desk. Perhaps I'll go back one day. Could I run it faster than I did back then?

Another finisher of that year's race, although much further up the pack than me, was Lizzy Hawker, who finished fourth and came back to win it in the following year.

While Paula Radcliffe had inspired my marathon dreams, Lizzy was the first woman who really inspired me to give the longer distances a go. She won UTMB an incredible five times – including on her first attempt, in 2005, wearing borrowed kit and having owned trail shoes for only a little over a week. With a PhD in physical oceanography, the former researcher with the British Antarctic Survey had spent weeks training on a manual treadmill strapped to the deck of the organization's ship before winning the IAU 100-kilometre World Championships in 2006.

Having grown up in London, Lizzy lived in Cambridge while completing her PhD but later stepped away from academia and moved to the Swiss Alps in 2007. The same year, she set the record for running the 320 kilometres (199 miles) between Mount Everest South Base Camp and Kathmandu, Nepal, in 77 hours 36 minutes.

Like Courtney Dauwalter's successes, Lizzy's were even more impressive as they came across many different distances and terrains. Also like Courtney, and Eleanor Robinson too, a strong driver for Lizzy was curiosity – to see different places, meet different people and discover more about her own limits and possibilities. In 2011, she set the women's 24-hour world record for running with 247 kilometres (153.5 miles) on a road loop in Llandudno, Wales, and improved on her Everest record with a time of 71 hours 25 minutes. The following year brought a second UTMB victory, as well as a win at the 100-mile Run Rabbit Run in Colorado. Later that year, Lizzy went on to set a new women's record at the 249-kilometre (155-mile) Spartathlon in Greece, finishing third overall. In an interview afterwards, she laughs at the confusion that ensued from having a woman on the overall – traditionally men's – podium.

I read Lizzy's book, *Runner: A Short Story About a Long Run*, years ago. It details her journey into the mountains, as both a runner and a person, after falling in love with them on holiday with her parents as a child. It's a joyful and inspiring read, capturing a deep love for movement and place, which becomes heartbreaking as the narrative explores the loss of self she experiences through six stress fractures that take away her ability to race, or even to run.

Lizzy set up her own race in the Alps, the Ultra Tour Monte Rosa (UTMR), as a quieter, wilder alternative to UTMB. I'd love to run UTMR, but it usually takes place a week after the UTMB races have finished, in September, after the schools have returned. Perhaps one day, when the kids are old enough to look after themselves, Sim and I will run it together. We have a lengthy list of such races and adventures planned.

For now, though, this visit to Snowdonia is supposed to be my first opportunity to run some of the race route; to get some steep, mountain miles in my legs; to become more familiar with simply being 'out there' – on my own in high, wild places. We drive through Shropshire and into Wales on quiet, Christmas Day roads, but by the time we arrive in Llanberis, closed-up and empty save for a few families out for a post-lunch walk, I'm not feeling great, with a cough that's been worsening for a few days. That night, after hours of coughing, I feel an ominous pop somewhere in my ribs.

The previous day, frustrated by inactivity and deciding the cough wasn't too bad, I'd stupidly decided to run the 16 kilometres (10 miles) into Bath to buy some last-minute Christmas presents. I'd intended to get the train home, but it was cancelled at the last moment, by which time I was already shivering from sitting on a cold bench on the platform. I got a refund on my ticket and set off to walk home, in what had become heavy rain. By the time I reached the house I was shaking uncontrollably. I spent the afternoon sitting with my back to a radiator, dressed in two down jackets and a woolly hat, still shivering. The thermometer, when I took my temperature, read 40°C (104°F).

And so, instead of the long runs I'd intended to do, on our first full day in Llanberis I find myself out with the dog, plodding along at a walk, my feet shackled in heavy hiking boots so there's no way I can sneakily break into a wheezing run and set myself back again. Despite myself I'm jubilant to be here, climbing the steep path up to the summit of Moel Eilio, following the path along the ridgeline, sucking in the air, the views, the dramatic, stormy light and stopping regularly to spend a minute or so coughing violently. From the summit we drop into Telegraph Valley, leaning into the wind down the final descent to the easy path that will take us back into Llanberis. During the race, this descent will be the last big one, and it's horrible: steep, grassy, rutted and pockmarked by many past feet struggling for purchase. I try to seek out the best line: should I make it this far, I want to give my battered legs the easiest ride. But there is no good line – it is all at weird angles, all gravity sucking me downwards into the col below. At least I know now that this descent is what it is: if needs be on race day I shall slide down on my bum.

For the two wet and windy days that follow I explore with the kids, climbing slippery, winding steps up castle towers; circumnavigating Llyn Padarn; seeking out halfway cafes for coffee and cake. Sim, unhampered by the virus, runs up Snowdon twice. Finally, on our third day here, the weather clears. I'm feeling a little better, coughing a little less, so decide to run the final stretch of the UTS course, again taking in the summit of Moel Eilio and that savagely steep, grassy descent. I want to run the route the race will take me back into Llanberis at the finish, so that on race day I can hold the knowledge of what it will be like to finish within myself over the many hours and miles beforehand. I want to feel a little of the tingle and thrill of finishing so that I can keep reminding myself, when things get tough, that this is what I really want, that it's worth all the pain.

I wear running kit this time, my feet feeling light and free and grippy. I make my way fast up the first big ascent, using poles to pull my way up and steady my balance as I go. At the summit of Moel Eilio I stop to take in the views – to the sea at Caernarfon; to the dark crags of Yr Wyddfa (Snowdon), its summit invisible beneath a heavy blanket of cloud; to the undulating skyline of the Nantlle Ridge; to so many summits I'll need to navigate during the race. *Bloody hell*, I think, feeling the twist of fear deep in my belly.

The wind is fierce at the top, snatching my poles and tearing at my hood. Aware of the speed at which my body temperature is dropping, I spend only a few minutes standing still before setting off down the long ridgeline, pleased to find my legs feeling fresh, my stride easy and efficient. Each climb feels hard but doable and doesn't stay in my legs beyond each crested summit. As I teeter my way down that now notorious descent to the good path into the valley, I can see the sun slowly sinking below the mountains to my right. I have just enough daylight left to get back to Llanberis and a fiercely bright headtorch if I'm delayed for any reason. The light softens the landscape, drawing a purple-gold veil over the mountains. Splashes of sunlight shine out against the darkening sky on some of the higher tops. I feel my mood soften with the light bringing with it a sense of deep calm, joy and peace. I can see no other human, just the sheer mountainsides rising to either side, the long, sure line of the path drawing ahead of me. I feel safe, nurtured almost, and as if I completely belong in this time and place.

* * *

Back at home, January blows in with more storms. More unprecedented high winds, torrential rain and flooding.

Training is hard, but I feel like I'm settling into a rhythm. I'm learning to accept the discomfort, the heaviness in my legs, the lengthy winter darkness that leaves so little room for running in the light. I weave around, jump, or simply run through puddles on the towpath, staying on the high ground above the River Avon, which has burst its banks spreading mud-brown water over the fields and parks. Trees that usually mark the course of the river now stand strange and stranded amid a choppy, chocolate sea. Even far from the river the fields are quagmires, sucking at my shoes on every step, slippery mud threatening to slide my feet from under me. But I realize with each day of training that these things bother me less. I am learning to tolerate, holding my mind in a state of neutrality, accepting and dealing with these occurrences rather than letting myself see them as difficulties. This state of mind doesn't feel like a conscious decision, but instead is arising out of simply spending hours and hours putting one foot in front of the other in whatever conditions I find myself.

One obstacle we're finding hard to deal with is the sheer amount of washing we're producing. With two children who enjoy playing out in all weather and two adults deep into winter training, we have become an efficient production line of wet, muddy clothing. A line of damp shoes parades along the top of the radiators at varying stages of drying. On the days I run twice I can end up with two full head-to-toe changes. It doesn't feel sustainable, but we've little choice other than to hope the wet weather doesn't last forever.

I try to mix up the training a little, reducing the relentless impact of running on my body. The kids are keen to go swimming and I realize that my body isn't in an acceptable state for public display after spending months doing only cold-weather running. I rush for the shower and make my way through the familiar ritual. The critical glance in the mirror, the tentative step on the scales, the brief oblivion of hot water on the face, the chores that make our bodies more acceptable to the world. I battle through the body hair of midwinter, removing all traces of it from my legs and armpits, then carefully trim the bikini line lest the horror of a stray hair offend someone in the swimming pool. For most men, hair maintenance is simply a practical consideration. For women it is weighty with expectation, repression and conformity. And yet, beyond the comfort of my winter clothing I can't shun its removal.

One Sunday in February I run 43 kilometres (27 miles), setting out from home and running along the towpath to pick up the Circuit of Bath waymarked walking trail. It's a new trail, set up in 2022 for a charity event, and I've spotted the signs often and wondered where it would take me – it feels like an adventure. It's lunchtime when I leave the house – a bit later than I'd hoped to get out – and I tell myself that I don't need to do the whole loop if I don't feel up to it. I can always turn around, cut it short, choose a more familiar route . . . any time I like. It still feels like a long way, especially on my own on a route I haven't done before. I haven't brought a headtorch and I don't know if

I can get round before dark. I don't have enough food and I don't know if any shops will be open late on a Sunday afternoon. The excuses and objections tumble about in my head. And yet my feet keep turning in the direction of the arrows; my body keeps moving forward, further and further from home, despite the nagging doubts. Eventually I reach the point when to turn around would mean running further than carrying on, and so I carry on, cresting Little Solsbury Hill in golden late-afternoon sunshine, running the final miles across fields as dusk softens the landscape. I return home enlightened. Something has changed. Other than Sim and perhaps the kids, no one else cares about or even noticed my long run around the hills surrounding Bath. But I spend the evening in the realization that there are so many things I could do if I stopped listening to the voices of fear. It's so easy to fall for the narrative that we can't do things – that our bodies or minds just aren't capable, so why bother trying? But those are excuses. They're the narratives that keep us in our places, at our desks, heads down, doing nothing more than what's expected of us. They're the narratives upon which so much of our daily existence is built – sticking to our lanes, keeping the giant cogs turning so that the very few, right at the top, get to achieve their dreams – if we're not careful, at the expense of our own.

7

TRIAL RUN

'I love the 100-mile distance because so much can
happen. Things can go wrong and there's time
to rectify it. Each one's so different – it's a proper
rollercoaster. There's never been an ultra when I
haven't wanted to quit – where I've not said I'm never
running again. But experience has taught me that,
other than a debilitating injury, there's nothing you
can't work through. I always say "don't shit quit!"
Because you never know until you try.'

—Debbie Martin-Consani, Winter
Spine and Lakeland 100 winner

It's early March, two months before UTS, and time to line up
for the first of my 'practice' races. I have three of these planned:
today's 53-kilometre (33-mile) run around Salisbury Plain,
just a few miles from home; the Snowdon Spring Crossing
in three weeks, for which I've yet to decide the distance I'll
run; and then a local, low-key race of 43 kilometres (27 miles)
in April. I hope that undertaking these longer training runs

as part of official races will make them more enjoyable than running them all on my own might be, with company, food and water along the way and perhaps even a finishers' medal (or mug, in the case of the Imber Ultra) at the end.

Imber morning dawns, as many seem to, after a mostly sleepless night. I don't know why sleep is sometimes so elusive. I do know that lying awake at 2am feels frustratingly pointless when a good eight hours would help with almost everything, from being a tolerant parent and partner to the post-run recovery and adaptation necessary for improvements in fitness and strength. There's little more annoying than the endless stream of articles on the importance of sleeping well to those who are trying everything and still failing.

Fortunately, I've had enough bad nights before races to know it's unlikely to affect my performance short-term. So, I put it behind me and focus on coffee and getting my kit together. I'm testing out some of what I intend to wear for UTS – my La Sportiva Mutant shoes with their super-protective and grippy soles; my favourite warm-when-it's-cold-and-cold-when-it's-warm merino top with long sleeves and thumb loops, which I've found great for those variable days when sometimes you need the full arm-and-hand coverage and other times rolled-up sleeves for maximum ventilation. I stuff a lightweight waterproof jacket into the stretch pocket of my running pack and pull the pack on, snapping the closures securely across my chest. Into the pockets at the front go a soft flask filled with water, a couple of energy bars and a small packet of chewy sweets. It's hard to predict what I'll fancy eating once I've been running for a few hours, but I know there will be more options at the checkpoints along the course.

We get the kids up and ready and feed them crumpets as a thank-you treat for not minding the early start. I chew my way through a slice of toast despite race-day nerves eclipsing any desire for breakfast. Eventually there's nothing left to do but set off. Making a coffee to take with me and drink before the start, I feel like I'm heading into battle. It's my first race for nearly two years and I'm not sure I can remember how. But there's only one way to find out.

Race registration is buzzing with chatter and warmly fragrant with nerves. My number is 8, which feels like a good one. I spend the remaining time before the start fumbling with safety pins, running through my kit to check I've not forgotten anything, making sure the route is ready to go on my phone and visiting the loo many more times than could possibly be necessary. As I emerge from what's definitely my last toilet trip, I bump into Zoe and Jen, a couple of friends with kids a similar age to mine, who are also running the race. We stand together at the start line, exchanging tense good lucks, jiggling with cold and nerves, willing the race briefing to be over so we can get on with the running. It's Zoe's first ultra and we've run and chatted together a few times before the race. She looks even more nervous than I feel, but I know how hard she's trained and how well prepared she is. I'm looking forward to seeing her at the finish. Jen has raced a lot before, including an ultra, but not since having her three children. I feel like we're all slowly emerging from something; discovering new, blended versions of ourselves – the self before and the self after children – and trying to figure out how this new experience works.

Though chilly, the weather is dry and still – just about perfect for ultrarunning. As the town crier tolls the bell to start the race I instantly feel myself relax, the pent-up pre-race energy dissipating into the morning air. We make a loop of the field first, then follow a narrow lane to a steep footpath that takes us up onto Salisbury Plain. From there it's a loop of the Imber Range Perimeter Path, staying high until we head back down the same path to finish. This is a military training ground, with tanks and signs forbidding photography and even a deserted village – formerly the inhabited village of Imber and now a mock-up for real-life sieges.

I don't stop grinning for the whole of the first ten miles. All around us, in every direction, the plain stretches away to the horizon; rolling, calcareous grassland cut away here and there by ancient hands into circular hillforts. The red flags are flying, meaning live firing is going on. At intervals, huge explosions echo across the landscape, a deep booming that fills the air and shakes the ground beneath our feet. It's unnerving and makes me jump every time. But not even the armed forces blowing things up can wipe the smile from my face; and I pop up the brim on my cap to let a burst of unexpected sunshine warm my skin. I'm so happy to be here, healthy and uninjured after so many Did Not Starts over the past couple of years. Sometimes it does all come together, I think, taking in the intriguing surroundings, the long line of colourful runners spread out along the trail ahead, the feeling of supple strength in my legs. And it really is worth it. I ring Sim and tell him it's all going well, delighted to hear the kids happy and playing in the background.

I'm still feeling good as I leave the second checkpoint at 24 kilometres (15 miles), waving thanks to the generous volunteers who refilled my water bottle and offered me snacks and words of encouragement. To any parent of young children, the aid-station treatment alone is a reason to run ultramarathons.

As I follow the way markers along a lane and turn onto the next stretch of footpath, I start to notice an odd blurry patch in the vision of my right eye. I ignore it at first, popping my visor back down, thinking it's probably just the too-bright sunlight and will soon vanish. But over the next couple of miles it gradually spreads, becoming an arching, scintillating pattern of black and multicoloured zigzags. Soon I can't see anything with my right eye, although the world still looks relatively normal through my left one. I decide not to panic. I've had this once before – a retinal migraine, which could be brought on by (among other things) exercise, caffeine, low blood sugar, a lack of sleep and dehydration. I think of the huge coffee I had to kickstart my morning after a week of insomnia, the single slice of toast I'd managed to eat through the pre-race nerves and the minimal amount of water I've drunk during nearly three hours of running. I've basically completed the tick list.

My first reaction is of frustration, even anger, with the thing. I'd been feeling so good – how dare a migraine come along and spoil it all? But other than the vision loss, I also realize I'm still feeling okay. I think of Courtney Dauwalter, who once ran the final miles of an ultra having lost most of her vision in both eyes. She didn't just give up because of a bit of temporary blindness, so why should I? I've also read somewhere that running can help migraines, so perhaps I can avoid the sick, headachy post-migraine phase I had last time I experienced this. I decide it's not ideal but nor does it feel like running is making things worse, so I may as well carry on.

An hour later, somewhere around the 32-kilometre (20-mile) mark, I can see properly again. I don't exactly have a headache, but I feel decidedly odd – spaced out, trippy, like I'm running through an altered reality. And actually, I think to myself, it's kind of cool. I decide to put some music on, to ride the trip for as long as I can. I haven't listened to it by choice since the 1990s, but I find M People's 'Search for the Hero' and hit play. Moments later, I'm immersed in Heather Small's glossy vocals, bellowing out the chorus to the empty fields and big skies. The combination of Heather and the migraine postdrome brings with it a wave of powerful emotion that carries me along like nothing I've felt before. It's like I've discovered a new and slightly terrifying 'monster mode'. Having run the first two thirds of the race conservatively, sticking to my pre-race plan of using it as a long training run without wrecking myself to the point of needing a week off afterwards, I'm now devouring the ground, roaring my way along the rutted tank tracks, the chords and lyrics of my teenage years suddenly heady with meaning once more. The electric ping of intense excitement runs through my body – I'm running as hard as I can and I cannot get enough of it.

The final hill goes on and on. It hurts but I'm almost enjoying the pain. I know Sim and the kids are at the top, at the 48-kilometre (30-mile) mark, waiting to cheer me on before I run the final downhill stretch to the finish. I'm still singing and dancing when I meet them, E and H running towards me, arms reaching, big smiles on their faces. I hug them and hand them a couple of sweets each from the bag in my pack, wanting to stop and ask them about their day but knowing I need to keep going just a little longer and then we can catch up properly.

'See you really soon!' I shout as we say goodbye. 'Love you! See you at the finish!'

And then, suddenly, it's like the party's over. I'd been so excited about seeing them, so elated when they'd appeared on the trail ahead. And now they're gone. The music's finished. That wave of . . . whatever it is that I've been riding for the past hour vanishes. I have only a couple of miles to run but feel deflated, alone and very tired. I grit my teeth and push on, telling myself there's 20 minutes left at the most. I try to stay focused, knowing how easy it is to trip over or get lost in those final miles when it's so nearly done.

Something I also need to do is pee. Salisbury Plain has almost nowhere to hide; there are no convenient bushes or areas of woodland to dive into. And I haven't seen a public toilet or a Portaloo since the start, more than four hours ago. Most of the runners in this race are men, who happily pee anywhere they feel like it, but it's not so easy for the rest of us. My bladder feels like an overfull balloon that's been bounced for hours. It's incredibly uncomfortable and I wonder whether I've done it any long-term damage.

Of course, it's not just women who benefit from regular toilets being available at races. Anyone with a dodgy stomach or GI condition might need them, as might the local population, who can't appreciate having their trails and hedges spattered with runners' excretions. While it seems like men getting it out in public is an oddly over-accepted practice in ultramarathons, there presumably must also be some men who'd prefer not to?

This is one of the many inequalities Sophie Power wanted to address when she set up SheRACES, a global network aiming to support female athletes. The ultrarunner, trustee of Women in Sport and mum of three set up the organization after a photo of her, taken by Alexis Berg at UTMB, went viral.

In the picture, Sophie looks tired, as you might expect for someone running more than 100 miles around Mont Blanc. But instead of taking care of herself, ready to continue with her race, she's breastfeeding her three-month-old baby while simultaneously expressing milk with a breast pump. A male runner reclines on the floor with his feet up, facing Sophie's naked breasts. It's a shocking image, capturing an experience very few have had. It wasn't an experience Sophie would have chosen, either. Having previously lost a hard-won place at UTMB after falling pregnant with her first child, she chose to run UTMB just three months after giving birth to her second. It was this experience that made Sophie determined to change things for the better.

'UTMB had an injury deferral policy,' she says. 'But not one for pregnancy. I wanted to make sure other women didn't go through what I had.'

Sophie has finished many ultramarathons, including the Marathon des Sables – 250 kilometres (155 miles) over seven days in the Sahara desert – and the 153-mile Spartathlon, as well as UTMB. She's driven, passionate and gets things done, whether that's in business, in running, or in campaigning for better provision for women in races. SheRACES is already revolutionizing racing for women, including convincing big races such as the London Marathon and UTMB to introduce pregnancy deferrals for women.

For Sophie, a woman's place is firmly on the start line. She's passionate about working with race organizers to make sure that races, and ultramarathons in particular – races we can do at a pace that works for us and our bodies, and that play to our unique skill set – are welcoming and well set up for female competitors.

'Ultras are supervised adventures. Especially for women who don't feel confident about doing these things themselves.

You get someone else setting out the course, food and drink provided, people to chat to . . . It's wonderful. And for mums it's such a mental break just to have to think about ourselves for a few hours. When I'm running, whether it's on a weekly long run or during an ultra and having that time and space to just focus on me – what my body needs, how I'm feeling – that's such a mental release. It's also about celebrating our achievements – something we're often not great at doing. And then going home and showing the kids your medal and saying, "Look what mummy can do – look what women can do." It's not being selfish – it's self-preservation. Building ourselves up so that we can be stronger for our day job, which is probably lots of jobs, including managing work and family. Lots of women, and especially mums, think they could never run an ultra, but I think it's about reframing what it takes to finish these events,' she says. 'As a mum, everything we do is training. Running after kids, the school run, being on your feet all day. That's training.'

We also talk about some of the issues women have raised as part of Sophie's work with both SheRACES and Women in Sport. These include safety – one woman had a violent ex-partner turn up on the course, having tracked her location using the race-tracking service, designed, ironically, to ensure runners' safety – and the language and imagery used.

'But for the most part it's inadvertent. The race directors are mostly men, and these are often issues that not only don't affect them, but that they're genuinely not aware of.'

Sophie is enthusiastic about the potential for ultras to

welcome women of all ages and abilities and, in 2024, worked with race director Huw Williams to create the inaugural SheUltra. A 50-kilometre (31-mile) non-competitive event for women, held on the beautiful Llŷn Peninsula in North Wales, SheUltra is open to runners and walkers, with no cutoff times, women-only aid stations, and the option not to have a name published on the participants or tracking list. The event raises funds for cancer charities – specifically those helping women living with cancer or supporting someone with cancer.

Sabrina Pace-Humphreys started running after her GP suggested it as a way of coping with post-natal depression after many years of struggling with anxiety and alcoholism. Her book *Black Sheep* tells her story of growing up in rural Britain, living with the constant backdrop of racism and a sense of not belonging. One of many powerful moments in the book follows Sabrina's decision to start leading a women's running group. 'Finding running in 2009 saved my life,' she tells me. 'And so, on that day when I took on a women's running group at my local club, even though I was filled with anxiety and self-doubt, at the end of that first session I felt whole. It felt as if everything I'd been through – alcoholism, being a teenage mum, racism and so on – had all led to that point, had all become a sense of purpose. I wanted to show women how they could find meaning through movement. And to give them that hour just for them. All they needed to do for that hour was move their bodies. And those moments of women who thought they couldn't run suddenly realizing it is something they can do; all these barriers – physical and perceived – all they need to overcome them is support – to feel safe and confident. Straight away I knew that was what I wanted to do.' Seeing so few people of colour in the sport, Sabrina also co-founded Black Trail Runners, a community and campaigning charity, in 2020 with the mission to encourage more people of colour into the outdoors via the sport of trail running. In an interview with Live for the Outdoors, Sabrina explains:

'We're called Black Trail Runners, but actually we're a space for whether you're a black person, a brown person, a white ally, however you identify, for those who want to see a more diverse outdoors, that wants to navigate trails and see people of all colours represented. Black Trail Runners is a community for you.'

Work that people like Sabrina and Sophie are doing serves to highlight the everyday inequalities so many people face simply by virtue of being who we are. The lower expectations that we learn to accept and live with from an early age, which are so entrenched we don't even notice them until they're either pointed out or fixed. Those raising awareness of these issues play an essential part in empowering those who live with daily inequality, prejudice and discrimination – as well as those perpetuating these inequalities, prejudices and discriminatory practices – to act against them. We all have our privileges and our blind spots; and recognizing the impact of not feeling or being seen and having our needs go unacknowledged should help us consider the effects of our actions (of lack of action).

Back at the Imber Ultra, having eventually found a hedge big enough to pee behind, I make the final turn and then I'm back at the field we started out from, holding the kids' hands as we run across the finish together. We stay and clap the next runners over the line, many of whom I saw out on the course. Then we go to the prizegiving to collect my trophy for finishing an unexpected third in the women's race. It's four years since I last ran this race. I'm four years older but my finishing time is half an hour quicker – a fact I'm pretty happy with. Back at the finish line I spot Zoe and Jen, also looking tired and relieved and surrounded by their children, and head over to them for hugs and congratulations. It feels so good to all be back here, sharing our tales from the day. The race has brought us closer, given us a shared experience: a battle that we fought and came through together.

At home, I reflect on the highs and lows of the race. There were many positives: the incredible women who finished in front of me (Jenny Crouch, the second-placed woman; and first-placed Una Miles, who's the same age as me and has three kids, and who set a new women's record, finishing fourth overall and beating me by nearly an hour); the camaraderie out on the course; the snacks; the friendly volunteers; the sunshine; my third place and feeling strong in the second half, running faster than I had four years earlier. And a few lows: my random blindness; the lack of toilets; and the fact that I hadn't found racing easy – I'd been anxious beforehand, made worse by the fact that I rarely raced. I'm glad I ran the Imber now, but there were many times during the last few days when I questioned why I was doing it, thought I didn't want to do it and considered dropping out and doing a long run on my own instead. The race had been a relative success, but one thing was clear: I needed to find ways to stop these doubts and negative thoughts creeping in and derailing me before I'd even reached the start line.

8

CONTROLLING THE CONTROLLABLES

'It was incredibly intense. It was the culmination of 60 hours of effort condensed into those final few minutes. I knew I had to sprint up the hill to get to the gate before the cut-off, but I also knew I had nothing left – I was completely exhausted. I had to dig deeper than I've ever had to dig before. I thought I might not be able to make it, so I made myself run faster so it was over quicker. I didn't think about what I'd do when I got to the gate or even try to decelerate when I reached it – every ounce of energy was focussed on simply getting to that gate.'

—Jasmin Paris, first female finisher of the
Barkley Marathons, multiple race titles
and records holder, vet

I t's late March and my recovery from the Imber Ultra, along with some longer runs during which I aim to tick off every hill within an hour of home, have been going well. It's time to head back to the mountains for the

THE PATH WE RUN

second of my practice races, this time the Snowdon Spring Crossing, where I've entered the 56-kilometre (35-mile) ultra. This means tackling 3,400 metres (11,155 feet) of ascent – a similar ratio of height gain to distance as UTS – and the distance is enough to be a good test of my fitness, kit and nutrition strategy without needing too much time off training to recover afterwards. The Spring Crossing also takes place on some of the same ground as UTS; along with a couple of other shorter runs I have planned for while we're in Eryri, this should mean some good time spent on the course.

We've booked a house in Beddgelert for the four of us, plus my sister Lucy, her partner Sam and my nephew and niece. The house is set over multiple floors and the four cousins explore at high speed, finding every nook and cranny, climbing into wardrobes, playing hide-and-seek and generally making the most of the place. It's the first time they've all been old enough to really play together without needing one of us on hand to supervise – my niece is the youngest at nearly three, Eva's the oldest at eleven, and the two boys are in between at six and eight. Eva efficiently and good-naturedly manages them all, her patience with her younger sibling and cousins only slightly waning over the weekend.

It's good to spend some quality time with my sister, too – we're close and talk most days but don't see each other enough. With the kids able to amuse themselves so much more, it almost feels like the pre-child holidays of the past, when we'd spend the days exploring and the evenings in conversation and laughter over shared food and wine. It's important to me that this trip to North Wales, which entails sitting in the car for four hours each way, isn't just about my race; it's also about fun experiences and special memories for everyone.

One morning, Sim and I take charge of all four kids so Lucy and Sam can get out for a run together – a rare occurrence in a life filled with parenting young children and running a business. They head out for a loop of the hills and return after an hour and a half full of smiles and laughter, aglow with post-adventure joy. Watching my sister, I can see that emerging sense of reconnection with a past self, the embodied remembering brought about by the experience of running in high, wild places. When I speak with her on the phone a week or so later, she'll tell me she's keen to join a local fell-running club. I'm delighted for her.

Sometimes I tell myself that running is just running – it's not that big a deal. But then why is it that we get so excited about the simple act of putting one foot in front of the other at a slightly faster pace than walking? I see the effects running has on those coming to it for the first time, or coming back to it after time off, and it's clearly far from simple. Far from just running. It's magic.

* * *

The race is scheduled for the Saturday of our trip. But late on Thursday night an email arrives to say it's been cancelled due to a poor weather forecast. For a while I sit and stare at the words. I think of all the planning and money that's gone into getting here, the trouble everyone else has gone to, the hours I've spent making decisions about kit, food and when to go along and register. I know that race directors must keep runners safe; and looking at the weather there is a chance of snow. But I'm still surprised at the finality of the cancellation. Before leaving home, I'd checked the weather and packed accordingly – March in these mountains is bound to be changeable. I'd packed a protective waterproof jacket, more substantial than my usual lightweight running waterproof, full-body warm clothing and some microspikes that I could pull on over my trail-running shoes if the ground was slippery with snow or ice. If bad weather is cause for concern, why hold the race in March?

But I also feel pragmatic about it: we're here, with my sister, surrounded by mountains – this is a trip that we probably wouldn't have got around to organizing otherwise. The money we've spent on accommodation and getting here means I don't have any budget for an alternative race; but there's nothing I can do and overall, it's fine. Once the initial disappointment recedes, I realize this is an opportunity to get out in the mountains and explore – taking in far more of the UTS course than I would have done in the race. Several shorter runs instead of one long one means I'll need less recovery time, too. Being out there on my own will also bring a different experience entirely to my time here. The nervous excitement I've felt about the race is replaced with a deeper anxiety – the weight of knowing I'll now be taking full responsibility for my decisions and actions. From the moment I start planning a run, I'll be responsible for everything: the route choices I make, the judgements about my ability and the risks I encounter, what kit and equipment I take with me. There'll be no race kit list or kit check to ensure I have everything in my pack that I might need along the way. No one will be monitoring my progress. But with this deepening anxiety and sense of responsibility comes a broadening of experience. Getting through the race would have involved following the flags that marked the course more or less blindly through the mountains; trusting the race planner and course markers to have got it right. While those participating in a race of course remain responsible for their own actions and safety, some part of that responsibility is relinquished to the organizers, too – that's what we hand over the money for when we sign up.

Racing is fun, but going it alone will be interactive, immersive and involving to a completely different level. It's always possible for things to happen that are out of our direct control, but for the most part the decisions I make – or don't make – will determine the outcome. Out in the mountains, particularly in bad weather, we can live or die as a direct result of our choices.

Each year, in England and Wales alone, Mountain Rescue teams attend around 3,000 incidents. In 2021, Scottish Mountain Rescue attended 660 incidents, of which 19 were fatalities. Some of these are the result of genuine bad luck – slips, trips and falls; the unexpected onset of a medical condition; rockfall – but many are the result of underestimating and/or misjudging the multiple potential challenges of being in exposed, remote places. Thinking about being out in the mountains on my own, I know I'll be as prepared as I possibly can. I'll plan carefully, take plenty of warm kit and safety equipment and let Sim know where I'm going and when I'll be back. But I still feel vulnerable, unsure how to quantify the level of risk I'll be letting myself in for. Even after several long, lone forays into the mountains over the past six months, I still find myself wracked with anxiety and uncertainty before such a run; I still sleep badly the night before and spend the hours before I set out crabby and unreasonable.

Adventure necessarily involves an element of uncertainty; it has to push us beyond our normal, everyday limits in order to be exciting and fulfilling. This is what I crave in wanting to be out running long distances in remote places – so why does it scare me so much? I wonder whether I'm overestimating the chances of something going wrong. Am I suffering from information bias, reading the grim and devastating reports of those who have been horribly injured or lost forever in the mountains and assuming this is far more common than it really is? I realize what I need is a voice of reason. To talk to someone who lives and breathes mountains and really knows what it takes to enjoy them as safely as possible. I need Keri Wallace.

Along with her friend and fellow runner Nancy Kennedy, Keri, a hugely experienced and successful mountain runner, who's also a qualified Mountain Leader and rock-climbing instructor, founded Girls on Hills for exactly this reason. 'Lots of women were saying to us "we'd love to do what you do; we wish we could do what you do,"' Keri says. 'And at first, we were a bit confused because we didn't think we were doing anything particularly amazing. But then we realized there's a misconception about what trail and hill running entails. We set up Girls on Hills because we wanted to get more women out trail running; to show them it's not as hard as it looks from the outside. And by actually doing it – taking women out and running with them – we learned masses about what women's fears were, what the barriers were, and we can tailor our courses to address them. Over the years we've learned what works for beginners, but also for experienced runners – those getting into ultras and fell running and skyrunning. Those are the most male-dominated areas, so it can be really hard for women to actually visualize themselves doing it. That advocacy side is now as important as actually running the courses.'

I've always visited mountainous places but, until I started training for mountain ultras, it had almost always been in the company of a man – usually a more experienced partner who'd take the lead with navigation and decision-making. Chatting with Keri brings home to me how much I'm learning about being in the mountains alone, as a woman, aside from the basic mountain skills and fitness. 'We hear that so often,' she says. 'But once you've cracked it, and you're happy out there on your own, it's a whole new experience. You're out there by yourself, making your own decisions – it's so different.'

Today, Girls on Hills boasts a team of incredible, highly experienced and highly qualified women, all of whom are passionate about helping others discover the joys of adventuring in the mountains.

Keri and I have followed similar paths since becoming mums, having chosen to work for ourselves in areas connected with our passion for running and wishing to share everything the sport has given us with others. Keri's kids are a couple of years younger than mine and it's clear from the way she talks about the future that she's just starting to get that sense of emerging from early motherhood; that (re)awakening of possibility, new flames springing from a smouldering fire. For both of us, ultrarunning offers a rare space in which we, as 40-something women, don't just feel accepted but are welcomed and even celebrated. Keri shares a conversation she recently had with legendary ultrarunner Nicky Spinks, who works with Girls on Hills, on the subject of getting older.

'She said to me, "Keri – I don't even know what you're talking about. You haven't even reached your prime yet!" And I was like . . . Awesome! I realized it's about playing to your strengths rather than just doing what you did in your 20s and 30s and comparing yourself with that.'

* * *

My second reconnaissance run in Eryri is the 16-kilometre (10-mile) section from Beddgelert to Rhyd-ddu. This will come at around 120 kilometres (75 miles) into the UTS race, and covers some technical ground, so it feels like a good idea to familiarize myself with it without the added complicating factors of exhaustion and sleep deprivation that I'll inevitably be dealing with, should I even make it that far into the race.

The weather's looking good as I leave Sim and the kids happily exploring around Beddgelert and follow the gently rising trails up the lower slopes of Moel Hebog, the first mountain on the route. From below it looks rounded and grassy on top – a kindly, benevolent sort of mountain – a gentle start to a run with over 1,200 metres (3,937 feet) of ascent and an airy ridgeline to negotiate near the end.

As I follow the winding, rising path up the mountainside I feel the sticky fog of pre-run anxiety evaporate into the warm sunshine of a perfect spring morning. It's peaceful – just the rhythmic crunch of my shoes on the trail, the click-clack of my poles, the calls of new lambs and old ewes and the mew of a circling buzzard. The views open up as I gain height – out across the village of Beddgelert, now far below in the valley, to Yr Wyddfa – Snowdon – and its range beyond. Other than a small group of picnickers I pass lower down, it's just me and the mountain.

My feeling is one of utter contentment. So far navigation has been straightforward and the trail is steep but not difficult. I have a full day of running in perfect weather ahead of me. The kids are happy playing in the sunshine. Sim has done his own long run. For once, I feel no guilt about leaving them for so many hours. But then, into this carefree wandering of my mind, creeps a warning voice.

You're not even at the top of the first mountain yet, it says. *Anything could happen later on.*

As usual, that voice is right. Never underestimate the mountains.

Before long, I'm lost in the middle of a wide band of rocks, searching for the elusive path that's marked here and there with stone cairns but not quite often enough for me to avoid a couple of poor route choices, ending up on scarily steep or loose ground and having to retrace my steps and try again. Eventually, I make it through the rocks, grateful for a mostly grassy slope to the summit plateau. At the top I celebrate with a few squares of chocolate, enjoying some unexpectedly coastal views down into the wide blue-grey sweep of Tremadoc Bay.

The next section takes me steeply down into a narrow valley before the next ascent, to Moel yr Ogof – home to the cave that is said to have been the hiding place of Owain Glyndwr, who rebelled against Henry IV in the 15th century. Then, after a long climb, I reach the infamous Nantlle Ridge, which I'll be hitting about 129 kilometres (80 miles) in on race day.

The ridge is a monumental feature of the landscape, a series of crests and waves and fins with a trail running along the top. The section we'll cross during UTS is one of the trickiest, climbing to the summit of Trum y Ddysgl and then traversing the rocky, knife-edge descent from Mynydd

Drws-y-Coed. There's a moment of commitment as you step onto this traverse, leaving the relative safety of grassy slopes and obvious trails behind and embarking on a steppy, scrambly stretch, picking your way through the rocks, hoping it's the right one. For the most part, the moves aren't difficult; it's just the sense of exposure and consequences of a slip that make it feel serious. My main concern is making a route-finding error and inadvertently straying onto more difficult or dangerous ground. Remembering to breathe, I go to my old rock-climbing trick of pretending the drop simply isn't there. I focus hard on handholds and footholds, concentrating fully on each careful placement and shift of bodyweight. About halfway along, a red-and-white rescue helicopter rises from the valley far below and flies right over my head. It's an exhilarating moment. And a stark reminder that things can – and do – go wrong in these mountains.

* * *

As I continue to train and expand the horizon of what I believe is possible – and indeed what I believe is normal – many other runners take part in many other races, some of which make UTS look positively pedestrian. The Winter Spine Race makes for compulsive viewing as its competitors tackle more than 418 kilometres (260 miles) of the Pennine Way in January. The notoriously difficult Barkley Marathons sees a record three finishers – only the 15th, 16th and 17th in its 19-year history. In April, my friend Kirsty, whose words about 100-mile mountain races I found so appealing when I was beginning my own challenge, completes the Northern

Traverse – 300 kilometres (186 miles) from coast to coast across northern England – finishing fourth woman and first in her 50–59 age group. I check the dots on the race tracker frequently, watching her make her way from St Bees on the west coast across the Lake District and the North York Moors, finally reaching the finish on the east coast at Robin Hood's Bay, where she's met by her German short-haired pointer, Gilbert. What an incredible adventure. I'm desperate to hear all about it.

'Running all night on your own in the cold is at best awful, at worst dangerous!' she tells me in a post-race email. 'The first night was horrible weather (clag, rain and wind over Kidsty Pike and along Haweswater), but I was with people so it was okay. But the second and third nights I was completely alone for the whole time and it was very cold (frost on ground) and with the tiredness and calorie deficit, plus moving slowly, it was just impossible to keep warm enough. I had five layers on (two down)! On the third night I could barely stay awake and had to sing/talk to myself all night, because I knew that if I did fall asleep nobody would find me for ages! I think that's my biggest learning point – how the cold affects you when compounded by other factors.'

Talking to Kirsty, and to many of the other women running ultras in their 50s and beyond, I realize I really am rewriting my own narrative of what it is to get older. It's exciting to see alternative ways of ageing playing out; women simply moving to longer, more multifactorial events where the advantages of pure physicality are far less important than the experience, self-knowledge and reserves of endurance and resilience built up over a lifetime.

Kirsty's been running for many years, but for many women who discover ultrarunning later in life it brings about a whole new world of experiences, of self-knowledge, of learning. At a time when the early stages of a career are over, children (if they have children) are more independent and finances are often easier, finding ultrarunning – and finding they're good at it – is a glorious distraction from the entrenched narratives of age-related decline. Finally, we have something that's just for us. A new project that takes our minds and bodies to places we never dreamed of in our younger years.

And then, right in the middle of this joyous voyage of self-rediscovery, the menopause hits.

In the UK, the average age of reaching the menopause is 51. For up to a decade before this many women experience symptoms related to the changing hormone levels associated with the menopause, known under the umbrella term of the perimenopause. Until I hit my 40s, the menopause felt like something far away on a distant horizon that didn't require worrying about yet. I'd never even heard of the perimenopause. But as I began to inch through my 40s the topic of conversation between my friends and me turned increasingly to this new topic – the next stage of our reproductive lives that we were all about to embark upon. Most women start to experience perimenopausal symptoms at around 45 and, like the menopause itself, the specifics of these symptoms and their severity are highly individual. This left us all with an uneasy sense of impending . . . something. What will it be like? Will we be one of the lucky few who barely notice it, or like the increasing number of high-profile women now speaking out about their nightmarish experiences?

The menopause is a huge life event, with potentially far-reaching and catastrophic results for women, their careers, their health and their families. Recent research has found that women experiencing at least one problematic menopausal symptom are 43 per cent more likely to have left their jobs by the age of 55 than those experiencing no severe symptoms, while research by Bupa shows that 900,000 women experiencing the menopause in the UK have left work. This suggests there's a problem somewhere in the system. As females, we have little to no choice over when or how we experience menopause, but workplaces do have options when it comes to accommodating female employees going through this stage of life. After all, most of us come out the other side well before retirement.

Several of the women I've asked for advice on running my first 100-miler have talked about the menopause. 'It's an ongoing battle,' one runner tells me. 'Over the last couple of years, I've found it's slowing me down. I find the achiness and the fatigue difficult. Starting HRT has helped with mood and brain fog, but I'm having to learn to be kinder to myself. If my coach sets me a hard session

I'll now switch it around if I'm not feeling good and do it on another day. I've found the experience of menopause horrible – really horrible. I think back to the years after I started running ultras – when I was 43, 44, 45 – and I was fit and fast and recovered quickly. But now I feel slower and older. No one told me about perimenopause until I was in my 40s; no one tells you you're going to experience all these symptoms and it's going to have such a detrimental effect on your life. I think there needs to be much better education, to help women prepare for what's going to happen.'

Every woman experiences menopause differently; and right now, for me, it's a complete unknown. Being careful with our diets and listening to our bodies when it comes to training, as well as having an invested GP with whom to discuss the pros and cons of hormone therapy are all good pieces of advice I've been offered by those who've made the journey ahead of me, but ultimately the details of when and how I'll encounter this next phase of life are yet to be discovered. It's comforting to know, though, that during and after menopause, while our ability to run fast may be impacted, our ability to run long may not be. I'm not yet ready – physically or emotionally – to run races like the Northern Traverse; the time, money and resilience it would take are far beyond me. But knowing that the option may well still be there even in 10 or 20 years' time is exciting. And, for the time being, I'm ever more inspired towards my own 100-mile goal.

There's a month to go until UTS. That's just over two weeks of training and two weeks of tapering – the process of reducing the training load on my body to allow it to recover and recuperate so that, in theory at least, I can stand on the start line refreshed and ready to go. I cannot imagine where the months have gone. It feels like only moments ago that the time I had available for training stretched out ahead of me like the start of the school holidays. Now that time is nearly all gone and I'm getting distinctly back-to-school feelings.

* * *

It's Easter Monday and the April showers are in full swing. Gale-force winds have been forecast for Southwest England. I've had what I thought was a decent weekend of training considering we're all down with yet another cold – five hilly hours covering around 39 kilometres (24 miles) on the Saturday and then a long walk with the kids and a 2-hour run on the Sunday. Now there's just an easy recovery run on the schedule. Over a second cup of coffee, desperately searching for a bit of extra motivation to get me through the door, I spot a photo on Instagram of two of the other women taking on UTS. Smiling into the camera, a perfect backdrop of mountains and blue skies behind them, the caption says they've just spent 2 days running 113 kilometres (70 miles) of the UTS course and will now be ticking off the remaining distance.

As I read the post, I'm hit simultaneously by two powerful emotions. The first is joy at seeing women running in the mountains, looking strong, happy, confident and like they absolutely belong. These women are my heroines – I've followed their running journeys, dot-watched their past races, cheered them on from the safety of my living room. I can still barely believe that I'll be lining up at the same start line as them in only a month's time. But the second emotion is a crushing sense of my own crapness. Suddenly, the void between myself and the real runners feels massive and unscalable. I've recced a total of 48 kilometres (30 miles) of the course, alone and anxious every step of the way. Although there were moments of utter joy and a sense of empowerment, looking back now, the overwhelming feelings I'd had were fear during the run followed by relief when I finished unscathed. The all too familiar wave of imposter inadequacy engulfs me, panicked words filling my head.

I can't do this. I'm not capable. I'm going to end up looking a total fool. I'm letting my family and myself down. All those people I've told that I'm running UTS . . . Some of them at least are bound to check how I got on and they'll see I wasn't good enough, wasn't strong enough; that I failed.

I find Sim in the office and pour out this general sentiment to him. He is searching for the right words to make me feel better when Eva, wearing her favourite unicorn dressing gown, wanders in on her way to the garden and notices my fraught state.

'Why are you upset?' Her face shows concern.

I reassure her. 'I'm not upset, I'm just . . . worried.'

'I'm not surprised,' she says. 'A hundred miles is a long

way. I'd be really worried if it was me.' And then she's gone, closing the door behind her.

Her words break the tension. Sim and I laugh. I'm able to leave the place of heightened anxiety and return to a more pragmatic state.

There's some advice from the world of sport psychology that I've heard many times over the years of running and racing: control the controllables. When you line up at a start line, you can't control what anyone else has done in training, or what they'll do in the race. There are loads of things we can't control – the weather, the terrain, other people. But there are also plenty of things we can control, like our training, the kit we choose and, to a certain extent, our mindset on race day. It's easy to obsess and worry about the uncontrollables, but it's also ultimately futile as they are, by definition, beyond our control. Doing the things over which we have control as well as we possibly can, however, will make a big difference come race day.

I continue to sift my thoughts as I get ready for my run, searching for the real issues, the deepest-seated fears. Apart from the objective dangers of rocks and cliffs and mountains, which I'm trying my best to ignore, I discover one that haunts me more than any other. This is a voice that tells me that I'll be timed out at an early checkpoint and someone will ask me why I'd ever thought I'd be capable of completing a race like this – why on Earth I'd entered in the first place. Races like this, the voice says, aren't for people like me – people with broken bodies and anxious minds who haven't done anything extreme for more than a decade. But having found that voice, I can also find an answer. How will I ever know if I'm the kind of person who can do things like this if I never try? By trying, even if I don't succeed, at least I'll have a better idea what it takes to get anywhere close.

Lunchtime on Friday 14 April marks 4 weeks exactly until I line up in Llanberis, ready to discover what I'm made of – when it comes to running 100 mountainous miles at least. My training over the 6 months since I decided to take on this challenge has averaged around 100 kilometres (60 miles) of running per week with more vertical gain – 'vert' as it's known in the ultra game – than I've ever done before. My recent weekly distance has crept closer to 129 kilometres (80 miles), with longer 'runs' – which actually involve running the flats and downhills and walking the uphills – sometimes exceeding 5 hours in a day. Because it all happens slowly and imperceptibly, it's hard to pinpoint exactly what's changed over the past half year; hard to be specific about the adaptations my training has provoked.

Back at the start when I'd looked ahead to my imagined self by race day, I'd seen someone hardened by months of hard graft. Someone tough and sinewy, a mountain runner, a distinctly different self. But now I'm nearly there I don't feel very different at all. I know the experiences I've had will have changed me, psychologically, physiologically and physically. I know my expectations of myself have evolved because of these experiences. I know that my shorter runs are now two hours long, and this feels entirely normal. I think back to my concerns about my knees during 50 kilometres (31 miles) of running in November and realize that those same knees do feel distinctly different now. Perhaps . . . just perhaps, there's a possibility I might be able to do this.

9

ROLLING THE DICE

'My hope for women is that they just try things and see – and not worry about failing, or not failing. Find the thing that fires you up and try it. Because why not? Because what's the harm in trying?'

—Courtney Dauwalter, multiple race winner and record holder

With three weeks to go until UTS, the colds are receding at last. I'm still coughing at night and first thing in the morning, but it's definitely getting better. Unusually, this bout of illness even took Sim down, but he tells me he now feels well for the first time in weeks. After so much uncertainty I begin again to wonder whether UTS just might be possible.

Today I'm planning to cover 48 kilometres (30 miles). This will be my final long run before I start tapering. I'm running the Bath Beat, a local annual long-distance walking event raising money for charity and popular with both walkers and runners. It's a non-competitive event, with distances ranging from 20 to 43 kilometres (12.5 to 26.5 miles), with well-stocked aid stations and friendly volunteers at regular intervals along the way.

Sim and the kids are walking the 12.5-mile route, while I'm running the 26.5. I've decided to set off from home, rather than joining them in the car, running the 6 or so hilly kilometres (4 miles) to the start. Once we're all out on the course, I'm hoping to see them at points where our two routes converge.

It's a misty morning as I cross the fields that mark the boundary between the outskirts of our town and the countryside that surrounds it. A pale sun dapples a patch of cloud, but other than that the world is softly submerged in a grey-white veil. I feel my body slowly warming up as I run, shedding the early-morning stiffness, delighting in running's rhythmic motion that carries me across fields and stiles, through woodland lush and green with bright spring foliage, before dropping to the river and then climbing steeply to the outskirts of Bath.

As I approach the start, walkers and runners in bright clothing thread their way along the narrow pavements, alone, in couples, or in small groups. Some are heading towards the start line, others in the opposite direction, already off on their day's adventures. The non-competitive nature of the event means we can set out at any time between 7.30 and 9.30am. It's all wonderfully relaxed.

After registering and receiving my number, I join a long queue for the start. The queue snakes around a large hall, which buzzes with conversation. As a solo entrant, and seeing no one I recognize, I stand quietly, just taking it all in. I notice many of the women are wearing close-fitting Lycra kit, while most of the men's clothing is a looser fit. I notice men appraising women's bodies, their gaze travelling along the line, carrying out the obligatory up-and-down assessment of each body before moving onto the next. It's a habitual, unconscious action, learned in adolescence and entrenched ever since. But its meaning is as clear as if it had been printed on posters around the walls of the hall: how do I rate you? Each body is measured up against an internal meter. Perhaps the specifics vary from man to man, but they're all informed by a set of standardized characteristics that every one of us has been indoctrinated to consider appealing and desirable.

Early that morning, I had dressed in my own tight Lycra running leggings. But then, after a moment's consideration in a squirming moment of anticipatory discomfort, I had taken them off again and pulled on my favourite pair of knee-length baggy shorts instead. I was glad of that decision now, rebuffing the male gaze as it sought to decide whether I met with its expectations.

The mist is burning off in the morning sunshine as I set out on wooded trails traversing the skyline, high above the city. Bluebells and daffodils sway gently in a light breeze. I'm filled with that familiar yet always unexpected warm swell of gratitude at being here; at being able to be here. For so much of the past 12 or so years, the simple act of escaping for 5 or 6 hours to run just wasn't possible. The sensation of being alone with nothing ahead of me for the whole day but trails and cake stops is both delightful and delicious and I wallow and luxuriate in it. For me, this is a spa day, a self-care routine, an only slightly guilty pleasure.

The Bath Beat is a self-navigated challenge and I check the map and directions on my phone regularly to make sure I don't miss a turning or checkpoint. Some of the checkpoints require a photo of the number on a lamppost or the name of a house, so they're easy to miss if you don't know exactly where they are.

I've run around this area for years, scouting out new trails in the Avon and Frome valleys, and yet there are many ways we follow today that are completely new. I love this aspect of organized self-navigated events – the sense of adventure and exploration, the balance of support and self-sufficiency. It's like a treasure hunt, only the prize lies in finding your way rather than at the finish.

At checkpoint three I gravitate towards a pile of cheese and pickle sandwiches, which are exactly what I fancy right at that moment. Four sandwiches later, I refill my water bottles, take a couple of biscuits to nibble on the way, then head back out onto the course. I'm following a long, narrow path across open fields, long grass to either side, when a hare emerges from the grass just ahead and stops for a moment, its face turned towards me, eyes meeting mine. It is a wise face, I think; far more structured than a rabbit's, with golden eyes below long, black-tipped ears. I feel a connection with the animal, a momentary linking of consciousness as we stand staring at each other. I can't describe why, but I have the strong sense it's a female hare and that, somewhere, her leverets wait for her return.

For a few seconds it is as if everything – hare, human, the world around us, time itself – is suspended. Then another runner approaches, heavy-footed, from behind, and the spell is broken. The hare turns and flees. I watch and marvel at her powerful body fleeing fast and fleet straight ahead along the path then cornering at the field's edge. I watch her skirt the field boundary and then disappear into the woods beyond. The other runner passes me and I push on again, feeling as though I've just experienced something precious, ancient, incomprehensible.

Women and hares have been linked in mythology across many cultures, often involving women – or witches – taking the form of the hare to spy, hide or run away. For the Celts, the hare was a sacred and mystical animal; a symbol of abundance, prosperity and good fortune that was treated with reverence and never as food. Shapeshifting hares of Celtic mythology could transform into the form of human women. One story tells of the warrior Oisin, who wounded a hare in the leg while out hunting one day. Following the hare as it fled into the undergrowth, Oisin discovered a woman with an injured leg.

The Celtic princess Melangell is the patron saint of hares. After escaping an unwanted arranged marriage, she took refuge in Wales's Pennant Valley, creating a place of peace and sanctuary for animals and people in need.

As I continue on my way, I feel changed by the experience, sensing connections to others by threads of myth and mystery, finding repeating patterns linked by landscape and stories, wild places and wild things.

The remaining miles pass in a gradually intensifying haze of heat and fatigue and the simple joy of carrying on anyway. I discover that waterproof socks keep my feet dry through the many muddy, boggy puddles formed in deep, off-road tyre tracks. I drink three glorious cups of tea in quick succession at a checkpoint in a village hall, where a few other runners graze on a generous buffet. Here, I meet Jose, a Spanish podiatrist, and we spend the next few miles chatting about our shared interest in foot biomechanics – a niche topic that I hadn't expected to find myself discussing a marathon into a run. Eventually, a couple of miles from the finish, we catch up with Sim and the kids. They're nearing the end of their 12-mile route, and Jose disappears into the distance, waving goodbye as he goes. I relish sharing the finishing stretch with my family. I'm so proud of my children, making it through 12 hilly miles and still – with the help of the regular cake stops – happy and enthusiastic. And I'm so grateful to Sim for supporting me in yet another running adventure.

* * *

A few nights after the Bath Beat, I wake with a strange, unbalanced sensation. My face feels numb, I can't hear out of my right ear and I feel sick and dizzy. I lie still, hoping it's just that I've been sleeping in a strange position and it'll all go away, but minutes pass with no change. I sit up and massage my face and ear, which seems to help a little. Eventually I go back to sleep and think nothing more of it. But the next night it happens again, and this time I can't get rid of the sensation. In the morning I'm still deaf in one ear and numb across that side of my face, with a feeling of absence as if I've had a dentist's anaesthetic.

After the recent cold and subsequent chest infection, one of too many picked up over the past months, I had made a pact with myself: if I stayed healthy I would go and give UTS my best shot. If I got ill again, I wouldn't be ready enough to do the course, myself, or my family justice. I was confident that, if I had these final few weeks to complete my planned training and allow my body to rest and recover, I'd have a chance of finishing the race. But this latest setback pushed that goal even further out of my reach. I thought of the time Sim and the kids were giving up to support me, the hours in the car, a missed cello lesson, the money we were spending on renting a cottage in Beddgelert for the weekend. I was painfully aware that if I showed up anything other than at my best, there was a strong likelihood I'd drop out and need to ask this of them all over again.

A spring race had always been a gamble – knowing how often the kids pick up colds over the winter months; the cold, wet, short days for training; the unpredictable weather. Historically I have struggled with spring races for these reasons. Statistics suggest that women are at a greater disadvantage when it comes to training for spring races, with dark mornings and evenings and sick kids disproportionately affecting our ability to run.

The following day, I head out for a walk with Renee, our dogs trotting ahead as we amble through the rain. She has just returned from two weeks racing in Nepal and is struggling to reintegrate into our hyper-connected world, already desperate to return to the simple way of life she has left behind. I find myself telling her I've decided not to run UTS, realizing only as I do so that I've made up my mind. Later, at home, I feel empty and slightly in shock. This is a race I have obsessed about, dreamed about, planned, prepared and trained for. It has been a constant feature of life for the past six months and more . . . and suddenly it's no longer there. Feeling like a total failure, I email the race director informing him I want to withdraw from the race and then I cancel our accommodation. Next I send a group email to all the ultrarunning women I've spoken to as part of my project to get to this start line – all those women who had wished me luck and generously shared their wisdom. And there it is: decision made.

For the next week, though, I am haunted by thoughts of the race. I question myself over and over. Have I made the right decision? Think of all those months of training. Perhaps if I just gave it a chance, lined up at the start, I might be surprised at what I could do. But my bad ear has also worsened, giving me vertigo and an inability to accurately locate or identify sounds. At one point I think I can hear the rumbling of thunder, but it's just my son, Hugo, playing Lego in his room upstairs. Out on an easy run, I think the dog has found a squeaky toy, but in fact it's a blackbird singing from the top of a tree. I watch people speaking to me, but I can't quite grasp what it is they're saying. It all makes me feel oddly detached from reality – a reality everyone but me seems to be inhabiting. And, worse still, I don't feel I can trust my own senses. This is not how I want to tackle UTS.

Yet still a part of my brain cannot leave the idea alone. I try to quieten the nagging voice, instead making a plan to come back next year in a shape that will enable me to do the race justice. Yes, I could wing it this year, hoping my symptoms clear up by the start. Yes, I could surprise myself and finish despite the lurking virus and lost training. But if I did decide to go for it against my better judgement and then failed to finish because of those factors – factors I'd known about in advance – then it wouldn't just be my pride at stake. It would be my family's shared time, money and physical and emotional investment in my dream. That feels like a precious thing to carry with me; and something I want to make absolutely sure I'm up to.

But with two days to go until UTS, I'm genuinely not feeling too bad. My hearing has mostly returned, the coughs that have plagued us for weeks have mostly disappeared and the dizziness I've been experiencing has almost gone. I check whether the cottage we had planned to stay in is still available and find that it is. Half-disbelieving what I'm writing, I send the race director another email, asking if there's a last-minute place for me. He replies that there is. Then we receive a commission for some work in Snowdonia, meaning we need to travel to the area over the next few weeks anyway – but we'll need good weather for photography. I check the forecast, which is looking absolutely perfect for both photography and running. The race starts at 1pm so we could leave early and make the 4-hour drive up that morning. I wander into the office, where Sim is working, and put the idea to him. Instantly he's enthusiastic, filled with belief in my ability to do this. I'm still not sure, but I'm about to get my answer.

Registration closes at 12:45, and we arrive at the start in Llanberis with half an hour to go. I've meticulously packed and repacked the bag I'll be carrying. Everything on the kit list has been carefully chosen, weighed, folded and allocated a place so I'll be able to access it easily during the race, which could take me up to 48 hours to complete. We're through registration and kit check quickly, a volunteer attaching a tracker to my pack before we head back to the car. Then it's a rush to get changed, apply anti-chafe cream to anywhere that has the slightest chance of chafing, attempt to lace my shoes exactly as I'll want them and pin on my number. With five minutes to go, I'm just about ready. I give enormous hugs to Sim and the kids and hurry over to the start line where the 230 or so other runners are already gathered, the MC revving up the crowd ready for the race to begin. I thread my way through the throng and into the back of the pen. Unlike the usual buzz at the start line of shorter races, everyone seems very quiet and still. There's no nervous jumping around or running on the spot – that would waste far too much precious energy.

There's not a lot of conversation either. This is clearly a huge undertaking for everyone.

And then we're off. I run with the still close-packed main group as we wind our way through the town of Llanberis and up to the Llanberis Path, the most popular way up Yr Wyddfa. I feel like I'm in a daze. I haven't had the nervous build-up, having decided so recently to take part. This doesn't feel like the culmination of so many months of training; it feels surreal, a sliding-doors moment, as if the half of me that made the snap decision to give this race a go is here while the other half is at home in Wiltshire, planning a more sensible alternative.

For the next couple of hours, we make our way steadily up Yr Wyddfa, passing the train, which shuttles passengers from the bottom to the summit and back, and tired hikers, some of whom look irritated by the long line of runners gatecrashing their Friday-afternoon walk. We pass the rearing rhyolite crags of Clogwyn Du'r Arddu, home to many of Wales's most famous rock climbs. Facing north, petulant and brooding, 'Cloggy', as it's known to climbers, stands clothed in a dark mantle of shadow despite a clear blue sky and bright, warm sunshine. I remember a day's climbing here, perhaps 20 years ago, thrutching my way up a crack running with water and slippery with moss, sweating with effort and fear. I think I'd far rather be running.

At the top of the Llanberis Path, most hikers would continue straight on to the top. The race ticks this off later on, though, and for now we drop off to the left, descending the Pyg Track, steep and rocky and wet with recent rain. I'd found the ascent pleasingly easy, but as we begin to descend my body starts to give up. I feel shaky, uncertain, lightheaded. People trot past me with ease as I use my hands to ease myself down the larger steps. I don't trust my feet, obsessing about the drop below. We make our way down and down, past the heart-shaped waterhole of Glaslyn, eventually reaching Pen-y-Pass and the first of 12 checkpoints. I'm relieved to have reached it and tick it off. I'm worried about how I'm feeling, so early in the race. I fill up my water bottles, eat a couple of chocolate biscuits and head off up the path, hoping things will improve.

I join a long line of runners and we slog our way up the steep, grassy, boggy lower slopes of Glyder Fawr, which becomes craggy scrambles higher up. I'm pleased again with how strong my legs feel on the ascent, but also aware of a throbbing in my throat and a tense, painful, swollen sensation building around my neck. I've also had a dodgy stomach since the previous day and a leaden discomfort sits in the base of my abdomen. I push on, towards the airy, rocky summit, still hoping all these nagging discomforts will simply go away with time. Nearing the top, I'm making my way across a rocky traverse when I'm brought to an abrupt halt. My left foot is stuck in a long, vertical crack in the rock, cammed in like a well-placed piece of climbing gear. I try to pull it free but it's completely wedged. I look at the long line of runners making their way up the mountainside towards me. The woman who is now waiting for her turn to cross the traverse looks at me quizzically.

'I'm so sorry,' I tell her. 'I seem to have got my foot stuck.'

She waits patiently while I pull and twist my leg, starting to panic a little but at the same time slightly amused at the utter ridiculousness of the situation. There's now quite a queue gathering – it's clear I really need to do something, and fast. I step up with my right leg and haul as hard as I can on my left foot, twisting as I do so. The urgency adds some much-needed strength and eventually my foot is freed and I can go on. As I continue up the steep scramble, I feel a twinge in the adductor muscles – those running up the inside of my thigh – of my left leg. I hope all the pulling and twisting hasn't done anything problematic, but for the time being it's not bad enough to stop me. I reach the rocky moonscape at the summit of Glyder Fawr and pause briefly to take in the views.

The next descent is on steep, bouldery scree that tumbles around us as we run. Runners behind me dislodge larger rocks that roll past, alarmingly close. We pass the tiny Llyn Y Cwn and then tackle the scrambly, steppy, boulder-strewn descent of the infamous Devil's Kitchen to reach Cwm Idwal and its gleaming lake, where grim legend has it that the unfortunate Prince Idwal Foel, grandson of King Rhodri Mawr, was murdered by drowning. The sense of constriction in my throat is now far worse and I can feel my glands swelling in my neck. It's not something I've experienced before and I can only think it's been brought on by the intense exertion of the climbs and descents combined with not having been fully recovered from the recent virus. My lower stomach grumbles ominously. There's a sharp pain in the left adductor muscles that I pulled on my way up. My waterproof socks have leaked already. I feel a rising frustration at feeling so bad so soon.

Reaching the end of the lake, I slow to take a sharp turn right onto a path that heads up to Bwlch Tryfan. As I turn, a sudden, sharp, burning pain shoots through the sore adductors. I stop, hoping the pain will go, but instead it gets worse, cramping and contracting the muscle until all I can do is crouch at the side of the trail and moan pathetically. After long minutes, the pain gradually eases and I try to run again; but within a couple of steps it stabs again, bringing me to my knees on the grass. I try again, fail again, attempt to reassure concerned passing runners that really I'm fine. Then I stop and sit on a rock at the side of the path. My stomach aches, my throat aches, my neck feels swollen and tender and now I have the worst cramp I've ever experienced. I look at my watch: I've run less than 20 kilometres (12.5 miles) with around 1,500 metres (4,921 feet) of ascent. Over the past months, I've run further countless times, higher many times and for longer multiple times each week. How can I have come all this way to do this badly? Even in my worst nightmares I'd got further than this . . .

And yet I know I'm done. If I'm feeling this rough at 20 kilometres, there's absolutely no way I'm going to make it another 20 – let alone the 148 kilometres (92 miles) left to run to get to the finish. Feeling thoroughly despondent, I ring Sim and tell him I'm dropping out. I ring race HQ and withdraw from the race. Then, shivering despite the warm afternoon sun, I put on all my spare kit and hobble down the path to wait for rescue.

I'd spent so many months wondering whether I might be able to somehow get around the course at UTS despite the struggles with illness and my fragile body. Now at least I have an answer. I know there are multiple factors that ultimately sealed the fate of this race. I'd anticipated some of these, but others feel random and unpredictable – like my waterproof socks leaking, which is something I've never experienced before even on long, very wet winter runs. I'd expected to be problem-solving my way round, but hadn't expected so many problems all within the first few miles.

I wonder whether I would have made it round if I hadn't been ill and if training had gone better; and honestly I'm far from certain. Well over half of those who start UTS drop out before the finish – this is no place for those who aren't thoroughly and specifically prepared.

Perhaps I need to face up to the fact that a mountain race like this is beyond me right now, with the limitations on my ability to get to mountainous places to train. I'd been pleased with how the climbs had felt, but the rocky, steppy, technical descents had caught me unawares and would probably have been my downfall however well everything else went.

Back at the cottage we've rented for the weekend I make the most of the unexpected extra time, hanging out with the kids at the river over two full days of glorious sunshine, eating ice cream and nursing my physical and emotional wounds. Sim also makes the most of it, heading out to run in the mountains, plotting routes and taking photos for work.

On our final morning, we all walk up Cnicht, known as the Welsh Matterhorn because of its distinctive pointed shape. The sun is bright and the colours bold. The kids are in their element, scrambling up the final steep section without a care in the world and seemingly oblivious to the precipitous drop – although I can't help repeatedly pointing it out. The rocky top is bathed in warm sunshine, so different from my previous visit during a recce for the race, when the visibility had been almost zero. We take summit photos, share summit snacks and soak in the views before heading back down and then for home.

In between these welcome, precious distractions I dwell on the race. I find myself endlessly ruminating, endlessly scrolling through Instagrammed photos of smilingly successful runners crossing the UTS finish line or standing brandishing medals, endlessly dissecting how things unfolded. I just can't accept that all that training, all that planning and preparation has ended like this. Could I have hung on a bit longer before quitting? Could I have suffered through two nights? Or even one? If so, why didn't I? I tell myself that I'm not strong enough, not fit enough, not brave enough for this sport. That this is a challenge I'm just not cut out to achieve.

Although some of the factors involved in my failure were definitely beyond my control, watching the race unfold over the weekend brings home to me just how hard 100-mile running is – how much mental and physical suffering this sport demands in return for the reward of crossing that elusive finishing line. I know that next time, even if I'm well, I'm going to suffer deeply in my quest to complete the distance. But surely that's the point? If it was easy everyone would be doing it. That's why I want to pit myself against this challenge – for the opportunity to take on something I don't know I can do. For the opportunity to meet myself head-on and overcome my desire to quit.

Like most failures, and horrible as it is, the experience serves as a good motivator, giving me some much-needed fire in my desire not to go through it again. It's a stern reminder that I still have time to put in a lot of good training and that I really need to make the most of every moment if I'm going to get to the finish of any 100-mile race this year. I give myself two days to wallow in my self-made misery, weighed down by an overwhelming sense of failure and uselessness. But, surrounded by all the good things – the kids, Sim, the dog, sunshine and nature and a body that is healthy despite (and because of) its refusal to run 100 miles – the darkness and weightiness soon start to lift. I pick myself up, dust myself off and prepare to go again. For now, at least, it's time to put UTS behind me and move on.

Earlier in the year, knowing how uncertain it was that I'd get to the UTS start line – let alone to the finish – I picked out a second 100-mile race later in the summer. Now that UTS is behind me, I focus all my energy on preparing for the Beacons Way Ultra 100, a full east–west traverse of the Brecon Beacons National Park. The park has recently undergone a renaming, back to its Welsh Bannau Brycheiniog, just like Snowdonia has reclaimed its Welsh name, Eryri. I love these changes. I love the novel sounds of the Welsh language, the challenges its different sounds present for us English speakers.

When my family moved to the Welsh borders from suburban London when I was ten, I remember being fascinated by the dual-language road signs, begging my friends to teach me words of the Welsh they'd learned in primary school. I remember that feeling of leaving behind a place so devoid of mystery and magic and finding myself in one where dragons, princes and giants dwelled and battled on lofty peaks and in fathomless lakes. My new home was a place crafted from stories and legends, where the lush greens of grass and trees stood out sharply against a silk-screen of distant mountains and hazy skies. Every day after school, I'd sit on the bus as it struggled up the long hill home, feeling the tensions and confusions of the day falling away. From the bus stop at the top of the hill above my mum's house, the distinctive shapes of the Black Mountains across the valley called to me. Forming the eastern limit of the Bannau Brycheiniog National Park, and the boundary between Wales and England, the Black Mountains include Sugar Loaf, the Skirrid, Cat's Back and

Hay Bluff; these names and the sense of calm and belonging they bestowed upon me brought me joy however bad the school day had been.

My mum still lives in the same house she did back then and I've returned often over the years, seeking comfort, refuge and reassurance after many and various life-related disasters. Every time I come back to this place, my home for almost half my childhood, the mountains enchant me as they always did. They are just the same, although I am, thankfully, different. It's perhaps unsurprising that I strongly associate the mountains with home, and with my mum.

I'm not the first to draw a maternal connection with mountains. Everest's Tibetan name, Chomolungma, means 'Mother Goddess of the World'. The name Ama Dablam, another famous Himalayan peak, means 'mother's necklace', with the long ridges at its sides being the arms of a mother (*ama*) protecting her child, and the hanging glacier between them being the *dablam*, a traditional pendant worn by Sherpa women. There's the Mother Mountain in Washington, DC; Mexico's Sierra Madre, the mother mountain range; and, in Eryri, Yr Elen and Carnedd Gwenllian, named after a mother and her daughter, a Welsh princess.

So, it feels fitting that, after the disappointment and slightly disastrous outcome of my UTS attempt, my next 100-mile race will be in these mountains that have always felt like home.

10

THE ART OF ACCEPTANCE

'Draw support from the people around you, the runners
around you, from the aid stations, your crew, people
anywhere, that's what they're there for – to help get
you to the finish. So, it's like you have a whole world of
people who are who are there to get you to the finish.'

—Diana Fitzpatrick, first female president
of the Western States Endurance Race

O nce I've emerged from the post-UTS misery,
I unexpectedly have the best week's training
of my life. During this time, I cover more than
160 kilometres (100 miles), running twice on most days,
feeling fit and strong and filled with energy. After a couple
of easy days following this mammoth week, I run the hilly
48-kilometre (30-mile) route from home that I haven't done
since I last felt this good – which was before that latest illness
descended and stole all the energy and resilience I so badly
needed for UTS. It's only now that I'm fully recovered that

I really appreciate how crap I was feeling in the fortnight before the race and on race day itself.

When it comes to long races, especially those in the mountains, when feeling terrible is part of what you sign up for, it can be so hard to tell whether what you're experiencing is normal for the situation. In my post-race dissection of everything that had happened I'd questioned myself over and over again – had I really felt that bad? Could I have somehow made myself carry on? But now, feeling so much better than I have done for weeks, I know beyond any doubt that I didn't have the race in me on UTS day. For me, part of the deal of running 100 miles is not breaking myself completely – I still need to be physically and emotionally available for the kids afterwards. If I'm a wreck for weeks, what message does that give them? I'm fully accepting that if I do manage to ever achieve that longed-for finish, I'll be hobbling for days, perhaps even a week or more. I may not run for a few weeks. But I'm not willing to knowingly risk hospitalization or longer-term problems. Running long, hard races when you're ill can impact everything from your kidneys to your heart and that really isn't part of my plan.

One weekend, not long after UTS, we head down to Dartmoor to stay with Sim's parents. For three days, the kids are kept happily entertained by their grandparents and nearby friends. Sim and I are free to run, arriving back to cups of tea and hearty meals. It's just the break we need. On the second day, leaving Sim doing some helpful chores for his folks, I head out on a solo long run. I take a pack and some water, but it's a hot day and by the time I reach Widecombe-in-the-Moor, only an hour or so in, it's already apparent I'm going to need more to drink. I stop in a shop and buy a can of Coke, drinking half and topping up my water bottle with the rest. At any other time, diluted Coke is a horrendous thought, but during a long, hot run it's one of the best things there is.

Feeling much happier about my hydration situation, I make my way up the steep hill out of Widecombe and onto the long backbone ridgeline of Hamel Down. It's a fantastic viewpoint, with great visibility in every direction, from the sparkling sea at Torbay to the tall radio mast at Princetown – a handy landmark on Dartmoor, which is often featureless and hard to navigate – and out across the rolling eastern moors to the Teign Valley, with its dense patches of woodland and patchwork fields. It is a glorious day: sunny and clear and vibrant with colour. Skylarks rise, babbling into the bluest of skies; fluffy foals watch me with playful curiosity; two big red deer cross the path ahead; occasional walkers grunt a greeting as they pass, except the two who stare intently at their phones. I cover around 32 hilly kilometres (20 miles), running across open moorland, over granite tors, through temperate rainforest and along a boardwalk in a nature reserve. I spot wild orchids, listen to cuckoos, watch buzzards circling and a merlin scything through the air. I get back to the house tired, dusty and filled to the brim with the whole experience.

I open the door and find the kitchen buzzing with the sounds and smells of supper being prepared. The kids greet me with tales of a day spent outdoors, playing tag with friends, doing crafts with Granny. Sim proudly brandishes the war wounds he's gained through a few hours of chopping up logs and building a woodpile. As I stand in the shower, luxuriating in plentiful hot water and that satisfying post-run joy of simply having stopped, I reflect that it really doesn't get much better than this.

* * *

While researching how to prepare for running 100 miles, I've seen a few recommendations for running an 80–100-kilometre (50–62-mile) race five or six weeks before the main event. Scouring the race listings, I spot the perfect candidate: a 50-mile race in the Black Mountains, close to my mum's house. This would also be a perfect opportunity to try out a long run on the terrain I'd be running over on race day. I type out an email to the race director, Elle Wood, explaining my project on women in ultrarunning. Within minutes she replies with an enthusiastic offer of a place. It's the day after my hot and hilly run on Dartmoor and I have five days to recover before the race.

Back at home, I try to eat and sleep as well as possible, taking a couple of days' rest to let my legs recover. I also need to sort out my kit. I keep everything for races in a big duffle bag, which has a compartment for smaller items like my headtorch, spare batteries, compass and power bank and a larger one for everything else. After UTS, I had put all my race food – gels, bars and sachets of baby food – in a separate bag inside my race bag to keep everything together. Now, though, as I pick up this bag, I notice something feels sticky. On further investigation it transpires that at some point since UTS a mouse has managed to climb into the duffle bag and help itself to my food stash. It has nibbled its way through five packets of super-expensive Supernatural Fuel, pooed everywhere and generally made a pretty horrible mess. Sim comes in as I'm standing looking at it all in dismay. I show him what's happened and, without another word, he takes the whole sticky lot outside and cleans it up, washing the packets that escaped mousing and returning everything to order. Yet another reason why I love Sim.

With the mouse business sorted, I set about organizing everything I'll need for the race. We'll be camping the nights before and afterwards, so there's all the camping kit to pack, too. Packing really isn't my forte. For some reason, I really struggle to work out what I might want or need at some unspecified future time. Sim is great at packing; more than that, he actually enjoys it. Over many years of trial and error, we now have a system that works perfectly: he packs everything except my stuff and the kids' stuff and we all pack our own. I still find myself sitting and staring at an empty bag with no idea what I'm going to want or need to wear in a week's time, but at least if I mess up it's only me that suffers the consequences.

Race kit, on the other hand, is relatively easy as there's a kit list to adhere to. I run through the list on the website carefully, putting each item in its proper place in my running pack. Waterproof jacket and trousers, spare base layer, headtorch and spare battery, mobile phone, power pack for charging my mobile on the go, hat, gloves, food, the means to carry 2 litres (3.5 pints) of water, foil blanket, first-aid kit, compass . . . I download the race route onto my phone, which I'll use as my main navigation device, and my watch, which will be my backup. I'll also have a paper map, which I'll collect at the start. As well as the mandatory kit, I add a few things I've learned come in handy on long runs: a small ziplock bag of wet wipes, a buff to wear around my wrist to wipe my eyes and face, my earphones, a small tin of Vaseline for easy on-the-go lubrication of chafing points, and a small tin of sunscreen. With these essentials all packed carefully away, I add extra food: some un-moused pouches of Supernatural Fuel energy gel and baby food, a few chewy sweets and some salty crackers.

I'm allowed a drop bag for this race – a separate bag that I'll be able to access at the 42-kilometre (26-mile) point – and to this I add more food, sunscreen, Squirrel's Nut Butter lubricant and a strawberry milkshake, which has always proved to be just what I fancy mid-race. Sim and the kids will also meet me at one of the checkpoints along the route, so I give them yet another bag of provisions. It seems like a lot of preparation for a 50-mile race, and I feel slightly spoiled at having so much support, but it's lovely to feel so looked after; and it's great practice for the 100-miler, which is what this is all about.

The evening before the race, we drive the hour or so from home to registration in Llanbedr. I feel a tingle of excitement as we pass through the landscape I'll be immersing myself in tomorrow.

'How are you feeling about tomorrow?' Sim glances over at me, perhaps wondering why I'm being uncharacteristically quiet. It takes me a while to sift through the various thoughts and emotions in search of an answer. It's not easy to sum it up, because on one hand I know this is just a practice race: there's no pressure to finish in a specific time or position; it's just about getting some good, hilly, relevant miles in my legs and testing out my kit and strategy for eating and drinking on the go. But on the other hand, I know it's going to be one of the hardest days I've ever spent running, with more ascent than I've done in a day before and only 16 kilometres (10 miles) short of my longest-ever run. I know I'll want to do my best, to push as hard as I can, given the distance, terrain and forecast hot weather.

'Fine, I think.'

As we walk through the door of the hall that's serving as race HQ, race director Elle is the first to greet us, giving us a warm welcome and introducing the rest of her team. Everyone's incredibly friendly as I go through kit check and collect my number and instructions for the morning. On our way out I exchange nervous hellos with a few other runners. Then there's nothing left to do but head to the campsite and try to get some sleep.

Thanks to a group of bikers who talk in loud voices late into the night, an enthusiastic dawn chorus and our pitch being on a slope, I barely sleep at all. At 5.30am I'm drinking strong coffee and trying to force down some breakfast that I really don't want but know I'll be grateful for in a few hours. At the start point for the race, I pick up my tracker, which also has an SOS button I can press if I need help. I pop this into the stretch pocket on the back of my pack, say goodbye to Sim and the kids and head out to join the other runners gathering at the start line.

It's 7am and already a glorious day beneath a deep-blue cloudless sky. I've slathered myself in sunscreen except on my face, as I can't stand it when sunscreen gets in my eyes. Instead, I'm wearing a cap, which I hope will offer enough protection. Music plays, mingling with chatter and laughter. I breathe deeply, feeling that familiar gratitude at being here, healthy and uninjured and with the support of my family. Then Elle wishes us luck and rings a bell and we stream through the start, following narrow lanes and then turning up the first climb of the day. For my legs this is a rude awakening and I quickly begin to feel the strain of the climb on cold, inflexible muscles. The climb goes on and on, but soon the views start to open out and it takes my mind off the slog. I catch up with another woman, Amy, and we talk for a while as we climb – about running, ultras, where we live and what we do. After a while she pulls ahead and I let her go, keen to pace myself over these early miles.

We drop into a valley that feels humid despite it still being early morning. The first checkpoint takes me by surprise, arriving sooner than I'd expected. I fill one of my bottles with a mixture of Coke and water, thank the volunteers and carry on with barely a stop. Soon, another steep climb brings us to the top of a long, horseshoe ridgeline, which curves to the right, gradually rising to reach Waun Fach, which at 811 metres (2,661 feet) is the highest mountain in the Black Mountains and the second-highest in the Bannau Brycheiniog. The sun is hot now, but there's a north wind blowing across the high ground, which builds in force as we reach the trig point at the summit. I'm grateful for the change of direction, following a path that descends gently then rises again, tracing the edge of the escarpment with views out across Hay-on-Wye and Builth Wells to the Cambrian Mountains beyond.

On the long, tortuous trail down to the next checkpoint, in a car park at the bottom of Hay Bluff, I run right into the remains of a pony, which looks as though it had at some point in the not too distant past simply lain down across the path and died. The empty eye socket in the skeleton head stares up at me, but the mane is still in situ. The whole effect is horrible and I shudder, letting out an involuntary sound of repulsion as I try my best to avoid it. The hillsides here are dotted with small herds of wild Welsh Mountain ponies, beautiful and elegant with their long, sweeping manes, gently curved faces and unusual colours. They lift my spirits every time I see them, making this encounter even more unsettling.

Sim and the kids are waiting for me at the next checkpoint. It's wonderful to see them. I'm only 32 kilometres (20 miles) in, and still feeling good, but their hugs and cheery encouragement are just what I need. I don't spend long there;

just enough time to refill my bottles, snaffle a couple of slices of watermelon and pop a packet of Mini Cheddars into my pack. Then I'm off on the steep climb up Hay Bluff. One of my favourite parts of the race follows, tracing the long, narrow spine of Black Hill, known locally as Cat's Back, with views across to rolling, rural Herefordshire. I know the wooded hill where my mum lives is probably in view, but I daren't take my eyes off the trail for long enough to look. I find myself in a small group of men here and we all chat companionably, sharing stories of our ultrarunning past and dreams for its future. I'm a bit sad when the stunning ridge running ends and we drop into the valley below, crossing fields and through orchards that are welcome with shade. At one point we run through a small enclosure containing two alpacas, one of whom bustles up to us and starts pushing us about. It's unclear whether the creature is being overly protective of its mate or overly friendly with us, but I'm glad I'm not on my own. It seems most interested in Paul, a topless Scotsman who clearly spends a bit of time in the gym, so I make my escape and leave them to it.

I'm still with the group as we arrive at Longtown, the biggest checkpoint on the route at halfway, where our drop bags are waiting for us. Most of the others sit down, taking their shoes and socks off, having a break from the heat of the day. I'm still feeling good, though, so I fill up my bottles, add another layer of sunscreen and swap a couple of used gel packets for some new ones. Then I fasten up my drop bag, say thanks to the volunteers and decide to carry on alone.

Just before I leave, Amy comes in – which is a surprise as I'd assumed she was still ahead of me. Amy had actually warned me about the attentive alpaca when we'd chatted earlier on in the race, as she'd encountered them on a recce run, so I thank her for the heads up as I leave.

From Llanthony Priory, in the next valley, we follow a section of the Beacons Way back up the hill to the main ridgeline again. It's the hottest part of the day now and I ran out of water a while ago. Suddenly I'm incredibly thirsty. I can feel my heart beating in my ears, my blood thick with dehydration. All I can think about is water. Why didn't I drink more at the checkpoint? Why had I been in such a hurry to leave without taking a big drink when I had the chance? I'd topped up my bottles but by that point hadn't felt particularly thirsty, so it hadn't occurred to me to drink more. Now, though, with both bottles empty and at least another hour until the next checkpoint, I am deeply regretting this. My mouth feels like it's stuck together.

A little further on, I'm sure I can hear the sound of trickling water. I think I'm imagining it at first, but the sound grows louder and then I find a stream of water flowing out of the hillside next to the path. I look at the map and see this part of the trail is edged by a series of springs. This means the water is probably fine to drink, even though I don't have a filter with me. Desperate, I take out my bottles and fill them up, downing the first two there and then. It feels incredible: the water is cold and sweet – I've never tasted water so good. Having been utterly despondent only moments before, I now can't believe my luck in finding these springs right here where I need them most. I refill my bottles again and pop them into my pack, then splash the precious water on my face and arms before carrying on up the hill feeling a million times better. Our need for water is so fundamental, yet one we rarely really think about in countries where safe drinking water flows out of every tap. It doesn't take long without it to realize how precious it is.

I'm still on my own when I arrive at a circuitous route to the foot of Sugar Loaf, which rises, steeply in places to just shy of 600 metres (1,969 feet). I'm 64 kilometres (40 miles) in and at this moment it looks more like 6,000 metres – an insurmountable problem that my legs simply don't have the means to solve. I let out a groan – I just cannot do this. But somehow, despite myself, I keep going. I'm not using poles for this race – I can't remember the reason for that decision – so I push my hands into the tops of my thighs on each step up the hillside, trying to give them just a little extra power. As I near the top I spot a photographer poised on an outcrop of rocks above me. It's just the reminder I need that I have a choice over how I let these challenges make me feel. It snaps me out of my misery and reminds me I'm here because I want to be; I'm fit, strong, healthy and running around in these beautiful mountains. It's hard because that's the point. I pick up my pace, smile – because there's evidence this enhances sporting performance – and power my way to the trig point at the summit.

Sugar Loaf is a wonderful hill to walk up with kids, as

there's a high-level car park, obvious trails to the top and some of the best views in the whole of the National Park once you get there. Even in my trashed state I take a moment to gaze out at the view – to the tabletop summit of Pen-y-Fan, the rest of the Black Mountains and the rolling hills of Herefordshire. I have so many good memories of this place, from climbing it as a child to several visits with our own children at various ages and abilities. Instead of the family-friendly way down, though, today's run takes us over the rocks and down the steeper slope. Only 16 kilometres (10 miles) to go. Maybe I can do this after all.

With just 5 kilometres (3 miles) left to run, I pass Sim and the kids and top up my bottles as I'm still struggling with dehydration and desperately thirsty. There's a final loop left to run, and then the finish. I'm feeling more upbeat as I head up the last hill. I look at the route on the OS app on my phone – soon there's a left turn, then the trail contours the hillside for a short stretch before taking another left from where it's downhill all the way to the finish. I put the phone away, grateful it's nearly over. I can't wait to sit down.

I turn left and follow a path that's at first clear and then seems to peter out. At this point, there's a tiny, niggly voice of doubt somewhere in my mind. I ignore it and instead carry on, eventually finding myself wading through a field of thigh-length grass. Then I reach a wall topped with barbed wire. This can't be right. I get my phone out again and zoom in on the map. At greater resolution, the answer suddenly becomes very clear. I turned left too early and am now well off route. I curse and stamp about and then wonder what's the best way to get myself out of this stupid situation. I can't believe I've messed up this badly after 77 kilometres (48 miles) of perfect navigation. I look at the map again – I can go back the way I came, which is now quite a way in the wrong direction and involves losing quite a bit of height, or I can head uphill and hope there's a way through and onto the path I should be on. I choose the latter, which if it works will be far quicker – but if it doesn't will waste even more time.

After more wading through grass, I eventually reach another barbed-wire-topped wall with a tree alongside it that I use to haul myself up. I then manage to climb over the wall without impaling myself on the barbed wire and drop thankfully down on the path I should have run to begin with. I'm so hot, so tired, so thirsty . . . I really hadn't needed the extra detour. And then onto the path from the right direction pops a smiley chap called Ben and we share the final downhill, chatting about the families and dogs we're looking forward to seeing at the finish. After more than 13 hours in the hills, it feels so good to cross the line and stop. I'm delighted to have finished third woman and eleventh overall.

For several days after the race, I feel oddly feral: driven by instinct rather than reason. My body tells me forcefully when it needs me to eat and drink and what it needs me to eat and drink. It is impatient, demanding and also tired. More than muscle aches, of which I have pleasingly few, I am tired. A leaden tiredness that means everything is slightly harder work than usual. At times when I'd habitually stand up I find myself seeking a place to sit. The heaviness that this tiredness brings is in every part of me: from the obvious places like my legs to parts of me I'm not often aware of, like my fingers as I type and my eyelids as I struggle to stay usefully awake past nine-thirty in the evenings.

After two days of rest, easy walks and sleeping like I've been knocked out, I'm feeling recovered enough to meet my friend Anita for a run. We cover a gentle 16 kilometres (10 miles), conversation making the time pass easily. My legs feel stiff for the first mile or so, perhaps from two days of unaccustomed inactivity as much as 80 kilometres (50 miles) of running, but this eases quickly as I warm up. When I get home I reflect on how my body has dealt with 13 hours of moving over rough, hilly terrain. I realize that, before the race, it was this body that I doubted – would I be physically able to get round? But it's clear now that my body was absolutely capable; for here it is, not only having finished the race but also having recovered enough to get out running again only a few days later. Those doubts had all been in my mind – a mind that seemed not to know my physical limits. My perception of what's possible for my body can be updated only by doing. I can't talk myself into confidence in my physical abilities: I need to keep getting out there and keep trying, regularly pushing at my perceived limits to expand and update them. Never before have I been so reminded that we don't know what we're capable of until we start working it out by trying. And then who knows where that might take us.

The following day, however, I notice a pain in the quadriceps muscle on the front of my left thigh. I decide to take another rest day to let it settle down. But the day after that, when I take the dog for a short, easy run along the river, the pain gradually builds until, by the halfway point, I can't run at all and end up having to walk a slow two miles home. I try not to worry – after all, I've just done a hard, long run, with some big miles already in my legs from the previous couple of weeks, so it's hardly surprising something's hurting. But the nature of the niggle bothers me – it's a very specific point on my thigh, which might mean something as innocuous as a trigger point in my overworked muscle but could also be something more concerning, like a stress response in my femur. It's odd that it didn't come on during the race, or even on my run two days later, but it now seems to be getting worse with use, not better like a soft-tissue injury might.

I'm aware of the pointlessness of catastrophizing, but it's hard not to listen to the 'What if . . . ?' I so want to get to the start line of my next attempt at running 100 miles healthy and strong.

It's then that I realize that is one of my main worries: I don't have any idea whether I can run 100 miles. Usually, when I want to see if something is possible, I'll look for evidence to support it. But currently, having never run further than about 100 kilometres (62 miles) before, I have no evidence whatsoever.

But where's the adventure if we only ever embark on

challenges we know we can complete? Accepting that stepping outside my comfort zone is one of the primary reasons I want to do this in the first place, and learning to live with uncertainty about whether I'm capable of doing it, are key to getting to the finish line. But how do I learn that acceptance? How do I stop myself catastrophizing about my inevitable failure – which will in turn guarantee that failure?

On the recommendation of a friend, I speak with Danielle Frake, a registered mindfulness practitioner. She isn't a runner, and hasn't specifically worked with runners before, but as we talk it quickly becomes clear that the mindfulness practice she teaches and the struggles I have with dark moments during ultrarunning sound compatible. Over and over again when speaking with women who triumph in ultras, it seems to be the ability to control spiralling, unhelpful thoughts that is essential to carrying on when everything's saying stop.

I wonder if mindfulness might be able to help me deal more effectively with the general life stresses, too – money, children, work deadlines, health and so on. However stressful life is, Sim rarely lies awake at night worrying about it, which in turn means he's better at dealing with life stresses. I, on the other hand, spend the small hours ruminating on situations and scenarios, finding myself tired and unable to deal with much the following day. I ask Danielle about these wider effects.

'Mindfulness practice is fantastic for sleep,' she tells me. Even if all it does is help me to sleep, that would be huge, I think.

Since a disastrous attempt at participating in counselling after my parents split up in my teens, I've always avoided any kind of talking therapy. Danielle is different, though. When the pandemic hit, she quit her busy, stressful job and retrained as a yoga instructor and mindfulness practitioner before setting up her own business. I love that when I come out with a string of jumbled thoughts and feelings she's able to summarize them all neatly and accurately within seconds. She constantly challenges me during our sessions, checking I'm keeping up with my daily mindfulness practice and journaling, picking me up on the language I'm using to describe how I feel and demanding more clarity and depth from my descriptions. More than this, she seems genuinely intrigued by the prospect of working with me on this project to run 100 miles and to do it as well as I possibly can – not from the perspective of beating other people, but for my own experience.

We agree to work together for the five weeks up until the 100-miler, with a final session the week after the race. It's a bit of an experiment for both of us, but one that feels as though it has a lot of potential. Danielle starts out by telling me about some of the core principles of mindfulness, including patience, having a beginner's mind, trust, non-striving, acceptance and letting go. I revisit the unhelpful thoughts that plague me during ultras, many of which centre around these principles. Impatience – the desperation to get the race done, going too fast early on. Not being open to new experiences and panicking because I haven't done this before.

Lacking trust in my ability to keep going. Obsessing about other people in the race and how I'm running compared to them. Frustration at small problems and irrelevant niggles and feelings. Dwelling on unhelpful thoughts and memories. I long for a mental space where I can simply experience a race without contesting with all these things – perhaps mindfulness might help me achieve that.

* * *

It's four weeks until the Beacons Way 100 and Western States weekend, with a women's field widely touted as the most stacked in history. Held annually in California, the Western States Endurance Run (WSER) is an institution in ultrarunning. It's the oldest 100-mile trail race in the world, seeing 300 or so runners making their way from Olympic Valley, near the site of the 1960 Winter Olympics, to the athletics track at Placer High School in Auburn. Along the way, they traverse the traditional lands of the Nisenan and Washoe indigenous people, crossing the high country, running through the notoriously hot canyons of California's Gold Country, crossing the Middle Fork of the American River and finally following the historic travellers' trails to Auburn. The course draws runners to it as it has a little of everything: snow on the high country, heat lower down, runnable trails and incredible support. Despite being considered a relatively fast route, it still takes in around 5,500 metres (18,000 feet) of climbing and nearly 7,000 metres (23,000 feet) of descent.

The global ultrarunning institution that today is WSER evolved out of the Tevis Cup, an equestrian endurance event that first soldiers, and then (more famously) former rider Gordy Ainsleigh, completed on foot. The first woman, Pat Smythe, finished the official race in 1978, although women had previously completed the course. It wasn't until 1985 that the race officially became a 100-miler, measured at 100.2 miles. For those who reach the finish line in under the 30-hour cutoff, there's a coveted sub-24-hour silver belt buckle or a sub-30-hour bronze belt buckle waiting.

Female participation rates at WSER have always been above average. Today, women make up around 23% of the field, considerably higher than many similar 100-mile races, a fact that's reflected in the race's finishing statistics. The race was an early adopter of the pregnancy deferral policy and, in 2024, announced an official policy for the inclusion of transgender and non-binary athletes, an area which has not been widely addressed in ultrarunning. In interviews after the announcement, Diana Fitzpatrick, race president since 2019, said their proactive, trust-based policy, created specifically for WSER and based on the best available evidence, intended to send a message of inclusivity to trans runners, refraining from being overly intrusive while also addressing concerns about competitive fairness.

In 1989, the legendary US ultrarunner Ann Trason claimed the first of her astonishing 14 victories at the race. Trason would go on to finish in the top 10 overall on multiple occasions, including third overall in 1992. Trason's record stood for 18 years until it was broken in 2012 by Ellie Greenwood with a time of 16:47:19. In 2021, despite hot conditions resulting in the lowest finisher rate for more than a decade, half of the top 30 finishers were women, with Britain's Beth Pascall taking the women's win in the second-fastest women's time.

But 2023 will rewrite the record books of women's ultrarunning history, starting right here at Western States.

From the moment the runners leave Olympic Valley on Saturday, the live coverage is the backdrop to our weekend. Courtney Dauwalter sets out at the head of the women's field and stays there all day. Her finishing time of 15:29:33 is 78 minutes faster than Ellie Greenwood's previous record, which had stood since 2012. France-based US ultrarunner Katie Schide finishes second, an hour and 14 minutes later, also under the previous course record time.

Courtney finishes sixth overall and her time is only 3.3 per cent slower than that of Tom Evans, the men's winner, who clocks the fourth-fastest-ever finish in 14:59:44. It's an astonishing race for women's 100-mile running, opening up a whole new set of possibilities for the future of our sport. Asked in her post-race interview whether she thinks her record will stand for many years to come, Courtney replies with passion that she hopes not. Instead, she thanks Ellie Greenwood for her previous outstanding record, which set a benchmark for ultrarunning women to realize what was possible in the sport, and says she hopes her record will be beaten soon by another woman. Courtney also characteristically refers to everything to do with her astonishing victory in the first-person plural – achieved by a 'we' not an 'I'. For her, it's so clearly a team effort, with her husband Kevin involved in every part of the process, from his meticulously organized spreadsheets to precision crewing that gets Courtney in and out of each aid station as quickly and efficiently as possible with everything she'll need for the next stretch of the race, including a joke to keep her smiling. Courtney often talks of ultrarunning in terms of pieces of a puzzle to be worked out and fitted together. When something doesn't go right, it's a piece of the puzzle that needs more work; and she and Kevin will work on it together. When things do go right, she makes sure everyone involved is fully appreciated. Watching Courtney's metronomic running gait, grateful smile and encouraging attitude as she makes her way around the epic races she undertakes, it's easy to think that she's somehow superhuman – that it must hurt her less than it hurts mere mortals. But the finish line tells a different story. After taking the win she pauses only moments before searching the crowd for Kevin and her parents. It's a deeply emotional moment that really shows the strength and depth of her foundations and her appreciation of this fact.

During her post-race interview, she admits she gave it everything she had, spent a long time as deep as she could chisel into her pain cave and the final 32 kilometres (20 miles) unsure whether her legs had it in them to take a single further step but filled with gratitude when they did it anyway. As if to prove her point, she then has to stop the interview in order to throw up.

If possible, the stories grow even more compelling as the day wears on, the merciless seconds ticking relentlessly towards the 30-hour mark. Pam Reed, at age 62 the oldest female finisher, crosses the line in 28 hours. A former world record holder in 24- and 48-hour racing, Pam has finished over 80 100-mile races and in 2002 won the infamous Badwater Ultramarathon, which covers 135 miles through Death Valley, placing first overall and beating the first male finisher by 1 hour 51 minutes. This year, a Western States finish is only the first part in a triple challenge for Pam, who'll be back at Badwater again in just over a week's time and then running the Hardrock 100-mile race 10 days after that. Courtney will be running Hardrock this year, too – an attempt at an epic double that few have achieved before.

The final 60 minutes at Western States is lovingly known as Golden Hour. This is when the real heroes cross the line, willing their broken bodies and minds to hold on for just those few last steps. It's an emotional time, with the highs, lows and everything in between that finishers have gone through over the past 30 hours written clearly across their faces. The final official finisher is Jennifer St. Amand who, surrounded by her supporters, crosses the line with just 21 seconds to spare. Every finisher is celebrated at Western States. Course records are published for female and male runners in 10-year age categories, with the oldest age group being 70+. In 2018, the year before she became Race President, Diana Fitzpatrick took the 60–69 record, crossing the line in 23:52:56. Western States was Diana's first 100-mile race in 2004 – the year she swapped from being a top-class marathon runner to an ultrarunner.

Aged 46, she crossed the line in 20:38:16, finishing fourth in the women's race.

'After so long road running, part of the beauty of running Western States was the unknown – taking the pressure off a bit,' she says, eyes sparkling as she remembers that first encounter with the race that would become such a big part of her life. 'My main goal was to finish. When I did, I remember lying on the ground wrapped in blankets – I felt like a burrito! I'd ended up finishing in the top five and the top ten got a spot to come back the following year. Someone came over and told me I'd get to run again next year. I remember thinking I wasn't sure I'd ever run again!'

Diana did run again, going on to finish Western States five times. She tells me her last one, in 2018, when she took the 60–69 record while being crewed by her family, was her favourite.

Every year there are runners for whom the clock does not wait. In 2023, one of these is 61-year-old Ashley Bartholomew, also known as 'Lucy's Dad', which is emblazoned on his supporters' T-shirts. Lucy has put her own incredible athletic season – which will include both UTMB and the Ironman World Championships at Kona later in the year – on hold to support her dad today. But time is running out for Ash. As the clock ticks towards 30 hours, everyone becomes focused on the story unfolding just a mile or so from the finish line.

Drone footage finds him out on the course, at the centre of a huge group of supporters, doubled over and barely making forward progress. His support team, which includes both Lucy and fellow ultrarunner Sally McRae, cannot physically assist him, but they're doing everything else possible to get him over those final, painful yards. It's hard to watch: the commentators are on their feet; the live chat is buzzing; the footage is at once heartwarming and heartbreaking; emotions are running high. After what feels like hours, but is, in the end, just two minutes too long, Ash limps and hobbles the final stretch of the athletics track and crosses the finish line. He's missed the cutoff but it barely matters – he's completed the distance. He'll get a finishers' medal, but no buckle.

I speak with Lucy in February 2023, just after her victory at the Tarawera 100 in New Zealand, which she completed in 17 hours 13 minutes. She's taking some time to rest and enjoying having a break from training.

'It's a great time to talk because I'm doing so little running!' she tells me, beaming into the camera, tanned from an Australian summer. 'I'm just running 30 to 40 minutes super easy – I told myself to just relax and find other things that bring me joy outside of training.'

Lucy radiates warmth and charisma. Despite only being 26, she's already a veteran of ultrarunning, an integral part of the ultra world. Inspired by her dad, who's supported her running every step of the way, she ran her first 100k through Australia's Blue Mountains. She joined Salomon's junior team at the age of 17 and has been a part of the sport ever since. At age 22 she lined up at her first 100-miler – the 2018 Western States.

'I had this mindset of "no matter what, as long as I get to that finish line I'm setting my PB" – so I felt like I couldn't lose,' she says.

With the pressure off, Lucy had a great race, finishing third in a women's race won by friend, teammate and mentor, Courtney Dauwalter. But the next year couldn't have been more different.

'Returning to Western States in 2019, I had this really competitive, comparison mindset against myself, and so, very quickly, I was not having the day that I'd had the year before. And then I wanted to stop. If I wasn't going to have that day – the day I had last year – I didn't really want any other day. In the end I managed to finish (fifteenth woman, almost two hours slower than her time the previous year) but I almost regret starting because I had such a negative mindset.'

This experience has stayed with Lucy and informs her approach to races even now. 'At Tarawera, I really wanted to have a positive relationship with the course and the distance. I didn't let negativity enter my mind. There have been some races where I've been running along already writing my DNF blog in my head, with all the excuses for why I didn't continue, but with this race I was determined not to let that narrative start.'

Lucy's only ever dropped out of a race once, when she was withdrawn from Western States by the medical team with a head injury. But, by her own admission, keeping going hasn't always been the smartest move, and her stubbornness has sometimes been to her detriment.

Running the 231-kilometre (229-mile) Larapinta Trail through the southern Australian outback in April 2021, Lucy ran herself into trouble. 120 kilometres (74.5 miles) in, she spent 7 hours without water, climbing over technical terrain in the heat of the day. The film documenting the run, *Running Out*, presents some uncomfortable viewing when, finally meeting up with her support crew Lucy is incoherent, uncoordinated, black-lipped and bleeding from multiple grazes and scratches, desperately trying to communicate her need for water to a crew that seems unaware of the seriousness of her condition. Footage shows her shaking as she tries to eat, drink and tend to her feet, macerated by river crossings. Right there and then, she considers giving it all up, calling it quits after an incredible 10 years in the sport and following a more normal path in life instead.

After school, when her friends left for university, got jobs and settled down, Lucy threw herself into running. The art of running and documenting her running life on Instagram has become both her career and her passion. Both running and the running community have given her many highs but also some lows. In a 2024 interview with human rights lawyer and ultrarunner Stephanie Case, founder of the not-for-profit organization Free To Run, which focuses on using sport as a tool for empowerment and education for women and girls in conflict-affected regions, Lucy notes how much more harshly she's judged as a woman compared with her male teammates. Scrolling through her Instagram feed, it's depressing to see the number of body-related comments she receives. Her responses are often polite but firm requests to avoid unhelpful comparisons.

But giving up running is never an option. She's driven by curiosity – of what's out there and what's possible. All these experiences, and her years as an ultrarunner, have brought with them maturity and respect for her body and the sport. 'I'm now gentler on myself,' she says. 'I won't push myself so hard any more, to the detriment of everything else.'

I ask Lucy how she keeps herself motivated in long races and challenges when things get tough and everything's screaming at her to stop.

'When you step over that start line you relinquish control of many things – like the weather, other people, falling over and so on. But, always, you've always got your effort and your attitude that you can control. So, your effort is things like eating and drinking, being smart in your kit choices. It's really hard to slow down enough at the start of the race, but you have to make yourself go slowly so that it's sustainable. The same with fuelling for the whole race right from the start. And then with attitude it's about staying positive, about not letting the negativity creep in, or problems that come up ruin your race. Effort and attitude is all we ever have, so we need to work with those and focus on what we can control and what we can control now.'

At Tarawera, Lucy's race food and kit didn't arrive in time for the start of the race. But instead of losing it over this last-minute curveball, she took it in her stride, and the result was a very positive surprise. Heading to the supermarket and stocking up on lots of the foods she knew she usually ate, like avocado on toast and quesadillas, she ended up eating lots of whole foods in the first half of the race and then moving onto gels later on. This approach flips conventional wisdom on its head, as many ultrarunners start out on sweet foods and then move onto savoury later on – but by this point, they're often too fatigued to eat proper food.

'It meant I was able to really nourish my body early on in the race, and then move to the bad stuff later on,' she tells me. 'It worked so well. I think there's so much still to learn about fuelling and nutrition, especially for women. Women are already crushing it in ultrarunning, but with better nutrition . . . just imagine! It's so exciting where we'll get to if we can get that right.'

What runners, and in particular female runners, should eat during prolonged endurance challenges is still a much debated and very under-researched area. A fact I was astounded to learn when, having read a vast number of often-contradicting opinions on the subject I turned to the research to find a 2023 paper in the well-respected journal *Medicine & Science in Sport & Exercise*. The paper was an audit of previous studies, undertaken by many of the leading scientists in sports nutrition research, including Megan Kuikman, Louise Burke, Kathryn Ackerman, Kirsty Elliott-Sale and Trent Stellingwerff. The researchers conclude that:

'The literature that underpins the current guidelines for (carbohydrate) intake in the acute periods around exercise is lacking in high-quality research that can contribute knowledge specific to the female athlete and sex-based differences. New research that considers ovarian hormones and sex-based differences is needed to ensure that the recommendations for acute (carbohydrate) fuelling provided to female athletes are evidence based.'

For the time being, I have decided to heed Lucy's advice, gained through many years of experimentation and working with the best in the sport:

'Basically, in ultrarunning, calories in is good! No one is every going to judge you for eating in an ultra – they'll just be impressed.'

My conversation with Lucy also gets me thinking about the level of bodily harm I'm willing to accept to achieve my dream of running 100 miles. How much discomfort, pain and even long-term damage would I endure for that finish line? How long am I willing to be sidelined from running, and possibly even walking, afterwards? How deep into what Courtney Dauwalter describes as the 'pain cave' am I capable of making myself go?

Aside from the obvious risks of falling, rolling an ankle and chronic soft-tissue injuries, there's evidence to suggest that ultrarunning may have the potential to damage our hearts, kidneys and other organs. A 2022 review paper in the journal *Sports Medicine*, 'Potential Long-Term Health Problems Associated with Ultra-Endurance Running: A Narrative Review', which is co-authored by Dr Nick Tiller, notes the growing body of evidence suggesting that ultrarunning 'may have implications for long-term health, particularly affecting the cardiovascular, respiratory, and musculoskeletal systems.' The review also highlights the limited data on female athletes, who may be at greater risk of some health problems resulting from ultrarunning 'due to interactions between energy availability and sex-hormone concentrations.'

I think back to my conversation with Nick. 'I've run 100 miles a couple of times and, while they were incredible, life-changing experiences, knowing what I know now, I don't think I'd do it again,' he'd said.

As a mother, as well as a runner, I have an extra responsibility – not to be so broken that I can't be there for my kids in a meaningful way, and not to permanently damage myself, or worse, in the pursuit of the arbitrary goal of running 100 miles. Yes, this means I won't push myself to the limits I've heard many ultrarunners talk about, but I know it's the only approach that's going to get me to the finish line.

11

MOUNTAINS OF THE MIND

'Be patient, be brave, believe.'
—Courtney Dauwalter, multiple race winner
and record holder

Summer's in full swing when I run the five miles into town to meet a friend after work, breathing in the sensations of warm afternoon air, wildflower-speckled fields and the suppleness and strength I feel in my body after a few easy days. We run back together, chatting the miles away, talking about her plans for running her first ultra, which is only a couple of weeks away now. Her approach seems to naturally encompass many of the ideas I'm learning from my mindfulness practice, including an openness to the experience and an acceptance of whatever is to come. I can't wait to hear all about it.

With three weeks to go until the Beacons Way Ultra 100, there's time for one last big weekend of training. One final push with the dual aim of getting to know some more of the Beacons Way route so I'll know what to expect on race day and providing my legs – and my head – with a reminder of what they'll need to deal with.

We've booked a campsite below the Carmarthen Fans, a row of scalloped mountains to the west of the better-known Central Beacons. This will be the ground I'll cross on the second day of my run, when I'll be sleep deprived and many miles in, so I'm keen to know more of what awaits me in those final 48 kilometres (30 miles).

We find a pitch and start unpacking, spotting some familiar faces as we do so, setting up camp in the next field. Robyn Cassidy and Trish Patterson are here along with race director Shane Ohly, to recce day five of the infamous Dragon's Back Race, which crosses the Bannau Brycheiniog National Park on its penultimate stage before reaching the finish at Cardiff Castle on day six. Covering 380 kilometres (236 miles) in total, with 16,400 metres (53,800 feet) of ascent, it's known as one of the toughest multi-day ultras around. The race has a wonderful history, having been won by Helene Whitaker (then Diamantides) on its first iteration in 1992, alongside race partner Martin Stone as the race was, at the time, run in pairs. The race wasn't held for another 20 years but, on its first rerun in 2012, Helene returned and finished – this time as a solo runner – first woman and fourth overall. This year – 2023 – Robyn, who finished second in the Arc of Attrition earlier in the year, will go on to finish as the first woman and third overall (one of four women to finish in the top ten overall) firmly establishing herself as a force to be reckoned with in ultrarunning.

This is supposed to be one of the quieter parts of the National Park and the campsite has a strict policy of zero noise after 10pm. But, as we finish pitching the tent in a gentle but resolute drizzle, there's a group nearby already warming up with a fire, music and beers. We eat our supper in the tent, drink tea and play a few rounds of Cluedo with the kids, then start settling in for an early night. It's been a perfectly relaxed evening, filled with some of my favourite things: talking and laughing with Sim and the kids, cooking outdoors, tawny owls heralding dusk. I'm looking forward to the good night's sleep I know will make the eight hours of running I have planned for the morning far more pleasant.

Unfortunately, sleep is not to be. The group gets louder and louder as the hours pass. Music that could have been straight from a 90s mixtape pumps unhindered through our canvas walls. Rough, drunk voices shout for more drinks and sing along tunelessly to Kylie, Bryan Adams and Roxette. By 1am I'm beside myself, verging on murderous. Sim and Hugo are somehow managing to sleep through it all, but poor Eva is also awake and suffering the singing. I'm still awake at 2am, but at some point after that I must have fallen asleep anyway, and the revellers must have finally called it a night, because I'm deeply asleep when one of many loud motorbikes that will pass by over the weekend wakes me up at 6.30.

Sim makes coffee strong enough to stand a spoon in and I sit wrapped in a down jacket wondering if I can apply it directly to my eyeballs. My head throbs, as it often does with sleep deprivation, so I take a couple of paracetamols and unenthusiastically ponder breakfast. I look around at the options I'd carefully chosen for the combination of calories and nutrients – muesli, yoghurt, nuts, berries – and my stomach reels at the thought of any of them. Then I spot the kids' box of chocolatey cereal – a special treat as we're camping – and tell myself it's in their best interest as I pour a large bowl.

Another coffee later, feeling slightly revived, I carefully fill my favourite Ultimate Direction running pack – the one I'll be using for the race – with everything I will need, or might need, over the day to come. It's a long run through wild and remote areas without shops or cafes. While some of the Beacons Way is waymarked, lots of it isn't; so, while I'll be predominantly relying on Ordnance Survey's brilliant online mapping, I also take a map and compass as a backup. You never know when a technical glitch might break the app, or taking a tumble might break my phone. As well as this, I take a survival bag, full waterproofs, a warm top, a power pack to recharge my phone, a Petzl headtorch and spare battery, enough food for a full day of running and two 500-millilitre (1-pint) bottles of water. I know this won't be enough water to last all day, but I don't have the space to carry more; so I also take a LifeStraw filter bottle, which will allow me to drink safely from streams as I go.

As well as the pack, I have an Ultimate Direction utility belt – a waistbelt that gives me more space for carrying food, allows me to carry my Leki running poles slotted into the elasticated straps at the back and – an unexpected bonus that I discovered early on – supports my separated abdominal muscles (thanks, kids), which is especially important on longer runs. I check the weather forecast and find that cloud cover is predicted all day. That being the case, in what will turn out to be a decision I'll regret, I leave my sunglasses at the tent and don't put sunscreen on – after all, I rationalize, I'm wearing long sleeves, long shorts and a cap so I'm unlikely to need them.

I say goodbye to Sim and the kids, arranging to meet them in somewhere between seven and eight hours at the western end of the Beacons Way. If I'm not there in nine hours, we agree, Sim can start to worry.

It's a perfect day for running – warm and cloudy with a cooling breeze – as I set out from the campsite and cross the main road, picking up the Beacons Way and following it along fields and overgrown paths towards the inviting, scalloped sweep of the Carmarthen Fans. The dog's excited. At home he's sometimes a bit ambivalent about our runs, dawdling, pausing often to take in the smells, on edge about threat and hazard, studiously avoiding interactions with other dogs. But he's a different dog in the mountains – freer to be himself. I know exactly how he feels.

Shortly before the climb begins, I meet a man running the other way. He looks fit and fast and I wonder how many miles he's done already today. He grins.

'Going up?' His soft South Wales accent reminds me of the boys of my teenage years.

'I am. How is it?'

'Lovely,' he says.

It's a steep climb to reach the top, where the long ridgeline of Fan Hir awaits – the stuff of running dreams. It's runnable yet interesting underfoot, holding my attention just enough while allowing an appreciation of the landscape that flows all around me. I pass a huge raven, perched on the edge, see the jut of its beak, the gloss of its feathers and then, as it pushes off into nothingness with a call like a growl, the vast scope of its wings.

The ridge is followed by undulating waves of hills – steeply down and steeply back up again. I'm grateful for my poles, which come into their own on this kind of terrain. I meet a few people, sharing cheerful hellos, but it's not busy.

The high point of the run, in more ways than one, is Fan Brycheiniog at just over 800 metres (2,625 feet), which has a trig point and stone shelter. The views stretch out across the northern edge of the National Park towards the Cambrian Mountains beyond. I imagine what it must be like here in bad weather – the utterly exposed nature of the place, miles and miles of uninterrupted grassland. Thank goodness I'm running here in summer, I think. How little I know . . .

* * *

It's two days after the Beacons Way Ultra 100 and the tears are coming regularly and uncontrollably. It feels like I've lost more than a race – it sounds ridiculous, but I am utterly bereft. The disappointment is visceral, crushing and utterly overwhelming.

This pursuit of ultrarunning is more than a research exercise, more than a test of endurance. This is a passion. This was a race I had worked so hard for, dreamed about so often, imagined crossing the finish line of so many times. And then . . . Then I threw it all away. Two days later, with this reality full in my face, I long for the ability to transport myself back to that moment.

* * *

Seventeen hours into the race, I'm sitting in a warm car in a cold, wet, dark car park, drinking tea. I've just crossed one of the trickiest parts of the route, with difficult navigation, torrential streams running off the hills, ankle-breaking tussocks, leg-swallowing holes and deep peat hags, black and ominous in the darkness. Ahead is all the ground I've run before. I should be recharging my phone, sorting out my kit and food and getting back out there. But I don't. I stay in the car, listening to my pacer telling me how worryingly cold we both are. She's run the past six miles with me and we're now sitting in her car while her partner sorts kit and makes tea. I'm incredibly grateful to them for doing this. But the warm, bright car; the comfortable seat; the reassurances I'm hearing about the sense and rationality of calling it a day right here, right now . . . they're all too tempting for my sleep-deprived brain that's spent the past 17 hours out in the wilds of the Beacons Way.

'Would Debbie Martin-Consani call this shit quitting?' I ask, trying to stifle my uncontrollable yawning. 'I can't face telling everyone I've failed yet again.'

'It doesn't matter what anyone else thinks,' she says, soothingly. 'It's your choice.'

I'm so confused. I am cold, despite wearing a merino base layer, insulated jacket, insulated waterproof jacket, shorts, waterproof trousers and a hat. But that's because the weather was so bad on Pen-y-Fan that we had to follow a diversion to avoid the summits in case someone got blown over the edge. Then, after meeting my pacer as arranged at 84 kilometres (52 miles), we got lost, blundered about crossing swollen streams heavy with runoff and then moved too slowly across a stretch of particularly rough ground. Perhaps once I get going again I'll warm up. I don't know if my pacer will want to do the next stretch with me as she seems even colder than I am, but perhaps I can link up with some other runners so I'm not quite so alone out there on the empty, spooky Sarn Helen Roman road in the middle of the night.

I need to talk to Sim. I don't want to make any decisions until I've spoken to him. I exit the car and walk around the car park until I find a place with a tiny bit of signal. I wake him up, apologize, explain. The signal's bad and he can't really hear me, but I manage to get the gist across.

'Can you get some sleep in the car? You've got plenty of time. You're tired. Have a sleep and then make a decision. Don't make any decisions until you've warmed up and slept.'

It's really good advice, only I can't sleep with people around. I'm shy about sleeping. I just can't do it in public, not even after four hours' sleep in the past two nights and

97 kilometres (60 miles) of running behind me. I tell Sim I love him. But he doesn't catch what I say. I tell him again, but the signal's dropped and he's gone. Anguish twists deeply and horribly in my heart. I'm so tired and so cold and, despite my crew and the checkpoint and a steady line of other runners moving past I feel so alone. More than anything, I wish that Sim was here right now, warm and competent and full of the right answers.

I know I need to be brave; to somehow find my way back into the race I've been part of for the past day but can now feel slipping inextricably away, the distance growing – a gap that will soon be beyond my ability to cross. I should put my pack and headtorch back on, be true to myself and my race and keep putting this story together, one footstep at a time. This is the moment I've been waiting for – the 'Who am I?' moment I've been thinking about for so long; the one I've known I'll encounter perhaps many times during a 100-mile race. I prepared for this feeling in my pre-race visualizations, made a plan to keep going at least to the next checkpoint – never quit in the chair, as so many of the ultrarunning women I've spoken to have warned me. But I'm dizzy with tiredness, existing on the edges of sleep, unsure if this is dream or reality. I'm weak and vulnerable to rational words in a place where rationality barely exists – if it did, surely no one would run 100 miles. So, instead, I go over to the car, open the door and get back in.

'Good decision.' My pacer looks relieved. I don't blame her – no one could have predicted how bad the weather would be in Wales in mid-July. It isn't her race, so neither is it her failure. I feel numb as I make one final trip across the car park to hand in my race tracker at the checkpoint, get a hug from one of the volunteers and then settle into the back seat of the car. Numb as we speed along empty, wet roads through sleeping South Wales villages. The car is filled with despondent silence and the smell of wet kit. The heaters are on full and I slip in and out of consciousness, the dull weight of sleep pressing me downwards. We get lost and have to backtrack, adding another half an hour to the drive. It's past 2am and we're going fast, too fast for the wet, winding roads. Guilt seeps through the numbness. I wish I wasn't here. I should still be on the trail – my trail, building my story. We hit a sharp corner just a little too fast, the fright jerking me into sudden wakefulness. And in that moment it's as if I've been snapped suddenly from the warm fuzziness of a dream into cold, hard, clear reality. *What have I done?*

The week before the race had been full of the usual challenges, all conspiring to stop me sleeping. I attempted a couple of afternoon naps, only I live in a house where the very sound of the word 'nap' will send the kids, dog, power-tool-wielding neighbours or nearby car alarms into a frenzy, leaving me frustrated and grumpy at having lost precious time in the vain pursuit of sleep. Two nights before the race, Hugo came down with a stomach bug and I got three hours' sleep. Then, as well as being tense with nerves, we got unlucky with our neighbours in an Airbnb near the start in Abergavenny and I managed only a single hour's sleep the night before the race. As yet another race-morning alarm shook me from longed-for slumber at 4am, I hoped coffee would get me through.

The start line was abuzz with friendly chat and nervous but smiling faces. I handed in my drop bags – one that I'd be able to access at 72 kilometres (45 miles) and the other at 127 kilometres (79 miles) – attached my GPS tracker to the strap of my pack and said hello to a few friends, including Kirsty Reade, who was there crewing the incredibly experienced 100-mile runner Allie Bailey. A few minutes before 6am, I said goodbye to Sim and the kids, hugging them tight and telling them I'd see them at the finish. Then I joined the group of 100 or so runners ready to head out and discover what lay ahead.

The rain began as we crossed the line and didn't stop all day. We followed undulating country lanes out of Abergavenny and I settled into an easy run, chatting with Claire, a doctor who was running her second 100-miler, and Allie, who'd done many, as well as recently winning the Wild Horse 322-kilometre (200-mile) race. While some things hadn't been optimal in the build-up to the race, I was here, healthy and uninjured. I felt a wave of gratitude at being able to start something so big and challenging with at least some chance of completing it.

By the time we reached the summit of Skirrid Fawr – the first climb of the day – visibility was down to a few metres and the wind was picking up. The early miles blend into each other, a blur of wet bracken, grey mist and enjoyable conversations with other runners. I'd chosen to wear my waterproof jacket right from the start and was pleased with that decision as I watched other runners having to stop to put theirs on within the first few miles. I'd also decided to wear waterproof socks, but it soon became evident that this wasn't such a smart move. After an hour or so of heavy rain running down my legs they'd filled up with water, which was unable to escape. My feet were swimming about inside them and every step sloshed loudly. Finding nowhere dry to sit and empty them out, I simply carried on, feeling the water working its way into my skin. My right big toe started to sting.

Eventually, I spotted a church and dove into the porch, making the most of an undercover space and a dry seat to see what was going on with my feet. As I pulled each sodden sock off it emitted a large gush of water, and when I wrung them out even more came out. I'd only been running a few hours and already the skin on the underneath of my feet was turning white and wrinkly. The skin was actually starting to fall off my sore big toe. Having no dry socks with me, I put the now-empty waterproof ones back on, laced up my shoes and headed back out into the rain.

By the time I reached the third checkpoint, a welcome undercover hall in Crickhowell at 42 kilometres (26 miles), I could feel there was something amiss with that big toe. It had been sore for a while, but I'd used one of the mindfulness techniques Danielle had taught me – focusing in on the painful area and 'breathing' into it. I reminded myself that

I was not my sore toe, that everything else was feeling fine. I was amazed how well it worked, the pain vanishing as if by magic.

In Crickhowell, the volunteers welcomed us in and one made me a cup of tea while I grazed on sandwiches and refilled my bottles – one with plain water and the other with my usual water/flat Coke mix. I took my tea to a chair at the edge of the hall and sat down to investigate my feet.

'Oooh that looks sore!' One of the volunteers, a smiley grey-haired woman, was looking down at my macerated big toe with a concerned expression. 'Give me a minute, I've just the thing.'

Twenty minutes later I was back on my way, wearing a pair of dry socks that had been magically produced and with a padded wrapping of super-soft lambswool around my toe. As the volunteer had promised me, it worked like magic, cushioning the sore area and protecting it from water and friction. Having trained as a podiatrist and never having encountered lambswool for foot protection before, I'd been sceptical. But, I reasoned, I could always stop and take it out if it got uncomfortable. I needn't have worried, though, as it turned out to be a brilliant discovery and something I've since added to my repertoire of footcare skills.

It wasn't just the toe that felt cared for, either. I'd been blown away by the kindness of the volunteers at the checkpoint. Sometimes, when you receive care from another person, it's clear they're doing it out of a sense of a duty, or as their job. But the care, compassion and feeling of being nurtured I experienced at each checkpoint were astounding – utterly wonderful. As parents, we spend a lot of time making things feel better for our children – offering them snacks when they're hungry, cuddles when they're tired or sad and a sticking plaster when they've got a sore toe. But so rarely does anyone do these things for us. Was this why people put themselves through the pain of ultras? To feel simultaneously and acceptably vulnerable and cared for in a world where we always have to be seen to be 'managing'?

As the hours gathered behind me, I experienced that merging of self with surroundings that only comes with time. There's a sense of wildness, both within and without, that comes from spending whole days outdoors, moving through a landscape, exposed to the elements. The rain had not stopped since we'd crossed the start line, but I'd become so soaked through that I felt a part of this, too. Though we descended every so often into places filled with people and cars, feeling like aliens visiting from another world, for the most part our route followed the high ground, tracing ridgelines and winding trails through pockets of woodland and fields where weathered ewes watched us warily as we passed. Sometimes I'd find myself inadvertently herding a few, watching their woolly rumps trotting along ahead of me, trying to be as unthreatening as I could so they might stop and let me pass.

On the approach to the path that skirts the high ground above Talybont Reservoir, I discovered one poor ewe that had become entangled in a barbed-wire fence. The unlucky creature was long dead, hanging upside down and in a gruesome state of semi-decomposition. But the expression on her face still clearly captured the horrible struggle that had filled her final hours. In my depleted state the scene hit me hard, and I found myself speaking out loud into the emptiness. 'Sorry . . . I'm so sorry,' I said to the sheep, tears mingling with the rain as I ran.

The Taff Trail runs for 89 kilometres (55 miles) between Cardiff and Brecon. It's designed as a cycle route, with some long stretches of enjoyable, flat cycling woven through the hills and valleys of South Wales. Descending from the hills, we hit one such stretch of the trail after about 64 kilometres (40 miles) of running. Underfoot it was flat but stony, unrelentingly hard and sharp on already tired feet. The trail was edged in on both sides by trees, so every mile looked and felt exactly the same as the last. I found myself toing and froing with two other runners – they overtook me as I walked a short stretch and then, when they'd slowed to a walk further on and I was running again, I passed them again. While we said little to each other, it was good to have some company on such a long, lonely stretch of trail.

Eventually, the Taff Trail brought us to the Blaen-y-Glyn car park at the foot of the long climb that would take us to Pen-y-Fan, the highest point both on the route and in the National Park, at 886 metres (2,907 feet). This was where race organizers had transported our first drop bags to, 72 kilometres (45 miles) in, and I'd packed mine with a dry sports bra, long-sleeved merino top and heavier-weight waterproof jacket as the wind and rain was predicted to be fierce higher up.

I hadn't realized this would be one of the checkpoints that was just a small shelter, open to the elements, with no dry space or place for changing. There wasn't much I could do about that now. I put my clean towel down on the muddy ground and took my shoes and socks off, standing on the towel to dry off my feet. A kindly volunteer held up a Dryrobe to allow me a little privacy, but my options remained facing into the tent, where a group of male volunteers were cheerfully exchanging banter, or out into the car park, where an unknown number of people sat behind rain-misted car windows. I chose the latter, hauled off my sodden layers and replaced them with gloriously warm, dry ones. I wish I'd had some choice words for the chap standing next to me, who made some effort to have a good gawp while I had my top off, but at the time I had other things to think about, like reapplying barrier cream to my feet before pulling on dry socks and shoes, chugging down a milkshake and refilling my bottles and food supplies. I'd also decided to pick up my Leki running poles here, keeping my arms fresh for the big climbs and descents in this section of the race. Stuffing my wet kit into a plastic bag and fastening the straps on my drop bag, I said a heartfelt thank you to the volunteers and set off up the steep steps towards Pen-y-Fan, which lay somewhere up ahead, blanketed in thick cloud.

The wind was fierce at the top of the ridge, pushing relentlessly at my body, catching my feet so I tripped myself up. Having found my poles invaluable on the way up, I now stowed them away as the wind made it impossible to place them. The rain stung my skin and hammered at the hood of my waterproof jacket. Visibility was down to a few metres in places, so dense was the cloud. The two runners I'd passed on the Taff Trail had overtaken me while I was changing at the checkpoint and occasionally I'd spot them ahead – two ghostly figures revealed by a brief clearing of the cloud, only to vanish again a moment later.

As I began the final approach to the summit of Pen-y-Fan, a figure, bulky in many waterproof layers, loomed out of the mist. After a moment of startlement I recognized it as the race director, Wayne Drinkwater. The battering of wind and rain made it hard for us to hear each other, but he put a hand on my shoulder and looked intently at me, asking if I was okay. I grinned and nodded and he seemed satisfied with that. The team had made the decision to miss out the summits due to the bad weather and I was to follow an alternative path that traversed below the main ridge until I could rejoin the main route for the descent. There would be another member of the race crew further on to make sure we all took the right path off the mountain.

Thanking Wayne, I set off again in good spirits. Though the weather was unexpectedly bad, I felt completely at ease in this environment, with all my protective kit, legs that still felt as though they could carry me many miles and a team of professionals looking out for us and making decisions to keep us safe. It wasn't that I had handed over responsibility for my safety; more that I knew I could look after myself and be confident I wouldn't be expected to do anything with a high level of objective danger. I felt such exhilaration in the freedom of this recognition, and gratitude for all the factors that had come together to create this moment – right here, in the middle of the storm, where I felt utterly peaceful and at home despite the inhospitable conditions.

It seems impossible, looking back on the race, that I quit just a few miles further on. I'd made the long descent from Pen-y-Fan, picked up my pacer at the Storey Arms car park and then, as night descended, lost my way in both my mind and body on the boggy plateau of Rhos Dringarth. Meeting my pacer, I'd taken my focus off the race, stopped managing myself, stopped navigating, handed over responsibility. And then, after descending from Fan Llia to the Sarn Helen car park, it was all over.

* * *

By the Tuesday after my failure to run 100 miles there's less passion in my pain. Instead of violent outbursts of tears there's just melancholy and moping. I decide I'm going to allow myself this. Today I shall fully immerse myself in the misery and get it out of my system. Tomorrow I'll move on and plan what I'm going to do next. It's the summer holidays, so the kids spend the day with friends while I drink tea, eat chocolate, sit writing in my favourite chair and go for easy walks with the dog. It does the trick. By the end of the day, I no longer despise myself quite so much. The reproachful thoughts are gentler and more forgiving.

Social media, for all its downsides, becomes an

unexpected source of support during this time. I've connected with several women who didn't make it to the finish of the race and over a few days we send each other messages of solidarity. We share 'what went wrong' stories and plans for our next attempt. We're united in the horribleness of being a DNF. It's an awful feeling when you've trained so hard, spent so many long days out on the hills and so much money on race entries and accommodation, all with one aim – to cross that finish line and pick up a coveted 100-mile buckle – and all you end up with are three letters beside your name on the race results. One of these runners was Allie Bailey, who also wrote about the difficult emotions she was dealing with after dropping out. But it brought home that the dreaded DNF can happen to anyone – even Allie, who's finished more than 60 100-milers, along with some longer and harder races than this one.

I speak with sport psychologist Dr Carla Meijen about coping with failing to finish a race, sharing my surprise at just how powerful the post-DNF emotions are. It's something she's familiar with, and that she's helped her clients get through.

'It really haunts you,' she says. 'It's hard to let go. Some people carry it around with them for a long time.'

Carla's book *Empowered Birth* draws on sport psychology techniques such as goal setting, imagery, positive self-talk, breathwork and mindfulness-based strategies to help women navigate labour and birth. She's not the first person to have drawn a parallel between endurance running and labour – my personal experience was of many similarities – but equipping women with psychological tools to help with everything from feeling we have choices around birth to coping with emotions and changes of plan is something I hadn't come across before but which made so much sense. Interestingly, Carla has noticed a similarity between the way in which athletes feel about not having the race they'd hoped for and women not having the birth they'd hoped for and felt she could use techniques effective in the first scenario to help those struggling with the second.

An academic researcher as well as a clinician, one of Carla's main areas of interest is around challenge and threat states in athletes, which she uses to help athletes avoid disappointing races by planning for the unexpected. The theory suggests that athletes can approach a performance situation, such as a race, in either a challenge state or a threat state, and that this state can positively or negatively affect the outcome. An athlete who believes they are capable of, and engaged with, dealing with a situation that arises during a race is likely to experience a challenge state, whereas one who does not believe they are capable of, and avoids engaging with, a situation is likely to experience a threat state.

'If-then planning can be so helpful, even if you have no idea what situations are likely to arise,' she explains. 'Even if it's as simple as IF something unexpected happens THEN I'm going to stop and take a few minutes to think it through before acting.'

I've tried and failed twice now at the 100-mile distance. I try to analyse the common themes of these two failures. There were differing external influences to each – the plague of endless viruses and some simple bad luck at UTS; and now torrential rain and some poor decisions around kit and strategy on the Beacons Way – but I can easily identify two other factors that substantially contributed to my decision not to carry on.

The first is a lack of sleep in the nights preceding the race. On both occasions, I'd struggled to get anywhere near enough sleep, let alone attempt the 'sleep banking' recommended by some researchers before a long race involving one or two nights. I'd say the one hour's sleep I'd managed to get the night before the Beacon's Way race after a run of bad nights was pivotal in my inability to think clearly and rationally about my physical state when things got tough, eroding my resilience and resolve entirely. I wonder if better psychological skills might have helped – if I'd started out with an if-then plan, would I have made a better decision in that dark, rainy car park after so many hours of running and so little sleep? I'm far from sure. I'd felt so ready psychologically, all that mindfulness practice I'd learned with Danielle ready to kick in when things got tough. But, when it came down to it, instead of enduring like a steadfast mountain – one of my favourite mindfulness practices – I'd simply dissolved into the rain.

The second takes a little longer to pinpoint. It's harder

to admit and harder still to trace back to its origins. But I'm afraid of the night.

Something about being awake in the depths of the night has terrified me for as long as I can remember. My parents were professional musicians, often working late into the evenings, returning in the early hours. Living in London at a time when IRA tensions meant regular bomb scares in concert venues, and even an actual bomb in a nearby military base, my dreams filled with little-understood terrors. Waking into the lonely darkness, the dreaded, fearful ache would descend, hollow and unbearable. I was also a nightmare for anyone who came to look after my sister and me, as I tried to make absolutely sure my parents never, ever left me again. Until my later teenage years, I rarely stayed away from home. Perhaps it's why I haven't spent a night away from my children for the past 12 years – partly because I don't want my children to feel the same way I did and partly because I don't want to feel it again myself.

At UTS, finding myself high in the unfamiliar, cold, hard rocky clefts of the mountains in daylight, the thought of being out there, up there, in the depths of the night, drew the first threads of emptiness from the depths of my mind. I couldn't imagine being alone, worn down by effort and fatigue, utterly vulnerable to those monsters I'd been managing by suppression since childhood. On the Beacons Way, though everything else had gone so much better, even despite the weather, it was the encroaching night that made the cold, the sleep deprivation and the hours to come suddenly unbearable and the warmth, light and safety of the car so irresistible. For years I've been using my children as an excuse not to spend a night away from the people and place that make me feel safe. But perhaps this isn't all to do with the children – after all, I've never had any doubts that they'd be safe and happy with Sim – and is almost entirely to do with me.

While a few elite ultrarunners are fast enough to run 100 miles between dawn and dusk, I'm not one of them. So, if I really want to run 100 miles – and especially if I want to run 100 miles somewhere wild and beautiful, and therefore hilly and time consuming – I'll need to find a way to manage this fear. I need to get comfortable with running through the night, rather than letting the fear take hold and simply running away.

Out on the Beacons Way, I'd got closer. I'd run through bedtime, through the hour when I'd have usually read stories, shared cuddles and gone to bed in the knowledge that my loved ones were close and safe. But I'd still only made it through an hour or two of darkness before I'd got scared and run for home. In the calm, bright light of day, all this irrational fear seems quite ridiculous – how can a woman in her 40s be afraid of the dark? – but it's played a part in enough failures now that I need to accept it's a real problem and do something about it.

I've had many good races, but it's hard to remember exactly what they felt like. It's always the bad ones that stick with you. The joy of good experiences is fleeting, yet the misery of the bad ones can be hard to leave behind. Even Eleanor Robinson, whose running career during the 1980s and 90s was so hugely successful, had bad days.

Eleanor tells me, 'I have several memorable races, mainly the extreme events like the Westfield Runs, Tasmania Run, the 1,000-mile race, Death Valley [Eleanor was the first woman to finish the 135-mile Badwater Ultramarathon], all of which posed many problems and have been well documented. The only really "bad" one was my second Firenze to Faenza 100-kilometre [62-mile] race, which was also a World Championship event. I was aiming to retain my world title. Cruelly I failed through no fault of my own. I remember the event as "The one that got away".

'The race started in Florence and the first 50 kilometres [31 miles] was a long, uphill slog which gradually got steeper as you got nearer to the top. I was told that I had a 10-minute lead at the top of the climb and, feeling really good, started on the descent. I had a good pace going into the steep downhill section but suddenly felt a massive push and hurtled forward to hit the ground with a horrible crack as my head hit the tarmac. I came to, face down in the road, hearing a familiar voice saying, "Oh my God, it's Eleanor." The voice belonged to Malcolm Campbell, who, with his wife Marilyn, was following the race in a car. They had seen me pass the top checkpoint and were continuing to follow the race. A group of folk were clustered round me and they had stopped to see what the matter was. It just so happened that I wasn't in the official British team kit: the proper uniform wasn't ready in time for our event, so we had been issued standard Reebok kit, who were the British team kit sponsors that year. Until Malcolm turned up, no one knew who I was. An ambulance appeared and I was dispatched off to hospital as I had concussion. It turned out that a female cyclist had ridden into the back of me, leaving a distinct tyre mark up the back of my leg. The disappointment of being taken out of the race is still keenly felt.

'This sort of thing should never have been allowed to happen. My dream was destroyed and I never got another chance.'

While Eleanor's DNF was not her fault, and she clearly couldn't have continued, I'm struck by the power of emotion that comes across when she talks about it. The one that got away, still raw and unresolved even after such a long and successful career. Thinking about my DNF alongside those of Eleanor and others who've shared their stories with me brings home how much the possibility of failing to finish is an integral and essential part of ultrarunning. The uncertainty of the outcome is all part of the puzzle and of the appeal. We shouldn't be afraid or ashamed of failing to finish a race. Because failing to finish is so much better than failing to try or, worse still, failing to dream.

12

NEW HEIGHTS

'No-one gets anywhere by having an easy life. You have to do hard things, or have hard things happen, in order to give yourself a chance to be strong. And the more hard things you do, the more you can look back on them and think "well if I've done that, I can do this too".'

—Holly Stables, former GB marathon
runner, multiple race winner

It's August and we're back in the Alps. The weather is fantastic and the mountains are calling. We're exploring a new area – Oisans – and I can't wait to get some hard training in, making the most of the two-hour climbs and the thin air afforded by an altitude over 2,000 metres (6,562 feet). If I can train consistently for the 6 weeks we're here, I'm sure I'll be ready to tackle 100 miles in mid-October.

We pitch our bell tent in a pretty campsite in the valley and excitedly plan our routes for the week. The first day, I race Sim and the kids up the mountain – they take the cable car and

I take my pack, poles and plenty of water and run/hike the 1,300 metres (4,265 feet) to the top. By the time we meet up, they've had a long, hot walk between cable car stations and I'm covered in dried sweat and dust. Seeking out the nearest of the small mountain lakes, dotted across the plateau, we sink our bodies gratefully into its delicious green depths. Then we all jump in a cable car for the journey back down – I get a free ride as a reward for my climbing efforts.

The following morning, I'm ambling along a flat path near the campsite, a relaxing walk in the sunshine with the dog, Hugo riding ahead on his bike. Suddenly, my foot hits a rock awkwardly and then I'm falling, my ankle twisting under me. I put out my hand as I fall, grinding it into the gravel. My body hits the ground hard. Searing pain shoots up from my foot through my leg. Then everything stops and I just lie there for a moment, sprawled on the gravel, dazed and confused.

When I look up, I find a woman, immaculate in running kit, peering down at me.

'Are you okay?' she asks in a French accent. 'I'm a doctor – a physician.'

I sit up. The doctor's looking at me with a concerned expression. Waves of nausea and pain make me dizzy. Hugo scoots over, a mixture of worry and horror on his face. It's an unwritten rule that parents shouldn't fall over, especially not in front of their kids.

'It's okay – I'm okay.' But I'm not even convincing myself. I'm embarrassed and in a lot of pain. I'm also in utter disbelief that, with a month of the world's best running ahead of me, I've potentially broken my ankle. I check myself over. There's a big, gravel-filled gash in the palm of my hand and I've taken some skin off my knee. I notice the poo-bag I'd been carrying is a couple of metres along the path. Then I realize Hugo and the doctor are still waiting. I can't sit here all day.

I get up, very gingerly putting some weight on my injured ankle. It hurts like hell, but it holds my weight. I take a few steps and smile at the doctor.

'Honestly – I'm fine,' I tell her. 'Thank you so much.' I'm so grateful for her kindness, her genuine care and concern. The fall had been unlucky – the result of a moment's inattention combined with a boot-smoothed rock – but landing at the feet of this lovely doctor was about the luckiest thing that could have happened next.

Satisfied that I'm not badly injured, Hugo speeds off to alert Sim about my fall. I hobble and bleed my way back to the tent, where I clean my wounds and patch them up. Over the next couple of days my ankle goes through various stages of swelling and colourful bruising. I wear my walking boots, well laced up, which keep it splinted and at least mean I can continue to walk in the mountains, even if running's out for now.

That week, a heatwave hits Southwest France. Afternoons on the campsite become unbearable once the sun is high enough that the sturdy hedge beside our tent offers no shade. So, we escape by cable car, flying effortlessly to the high plateau at 2,100 metres (6,890 feet). Here we find mountain breezes to cool our skin, swim in the lakes and follow trails that wind through alpine pastures fragrant with bilberry and juniper. The bilberries – *myrtilles* in French – are at their point of perfect summer ripeness: plump, dark and sweet. It takes us hours to walk just a couple of miles between cable-car stations with the regular stops for grazing. It's utterly idyllic, and for the most part keeps my mind off my ankle. On our last day in Oisans, we sit outside a high *refuge* and drink extortionately priced Coke from frosty glass bottles, breathing in the vast views that reach to the Écrins National Park, the mountains still dotted with patches of snow despite the heat.

From Oisans we move north to the Belledonne mountains, which form an Alpine backdrop to the city of Grenoble. Our base is a pretty gite nestled in a remote valley, and Sim is due to run the local 80-kilometre (50-mile) ultramarathon over the weekend. Only things don't quite go to plan.

First the warm, sunny weather breaks and we watch the most awe-inspiring storm light up the sky and the mountains all around us. At one point, thinking the storm has finished, I take the opportunity to pop to the toilet, only for the loudest crack of thunder to explode right behind me. If it wasn't so terrifying it would be funny. As it is, it's an ominous portent of things to come.

With more storms forecast, increasing the dangers of being high in the mountains, we receive the news that the race has been cancelled. In the end, he's able to switch his place to the shorter Skyrace, which is still scheduled to happen. It's a savage 21 kilometres (13 miles), 2,000 metres

(6,562 feet) straight up the mountain and then 2,000 metres back down again.

The race goes well, although afterwards Sim tells me he's not feeling great. The following day, we all come down with a stomach bug. We lock ourselves in our apartment and wait it out, doing our best to look after the kids despite feeling terrible ourselves. It's such a waste of our precious few days in the area, but for the most part I'm feeling too rough to care.

At last, we're all well enough to escape. Feeling weak and still slightly untrusting of our bodies, we make our way over to Les Contamines, a mountain village close to Chamonix. It's UTMB week, and both the women's and men's fields are stacked with big-name runners. I can't wait to cheer everyone through the village, which lies 32 kilometres (20 miles) from the race start; night will be falling as the runners come through, with more than 129 kilometres (80 miles) still to go to the finish.

Eva takes part in one of the UTMB Minis – shorter races for kids aged between two and thirteen held in Les Contamines and several other villages that dot the famous loop of Mont Blanc during race week. It's wonderfully local, with an enthusiastic MC, 80s classics blasting from portable speakers and local mums handling registration and giving out goody bags to finishers. Eva's one of the youngest in the oldest age group and will be running the furthest distance of 2.5 kilometres (1.6 miles) over two laps with two big hills. I admire her composure at the start, waiting patiently for all the other races to happen, cheering the two-year-olds holding their parents' hands for a lap of the field and watching the more fiercely competitive races for older children. I scope out the competition she'll face, including girls much taller than she is. But she seems unbothered, focusing on her race plan. Whatever happens, I'm so proud already.

The gun goes off and a long stream of 12- and 13-year-olds heads out on the first loop of the local woods and park. When they pass us after the first loop, Eva's in third or fourth place. We scream encouragement as she runs past, still looking fresh and in control. We make our way to the finish line and cheer the first few boys through. Then, the first girl arrives – she must be a foot taller than Eva and is a powerful runner. She could also be nearly two years older, I think, which at this stage makes a big difference. But then we spot her, powering along the finishing strait, giving it everything, in second place but with the third-placed girl only a few paces back. Eva manages to hold on, crossing the finish line in second, and we run over to where she lies on the grass, catching her breath. We couldn't be more proud of her.

That evening, over celebratory pizza, I think back on the day – on this event that puts families at its heart and champions and enables the future generation of runners. It's such an important part of UTMB week for the local villages; and yet hardly anyone outside the villages seems to know about the Minis. It's heartwarming and true to the original spirit of the event and I love it.

As evening falls on UTMB day, we wait for the first runners in the gathering gloom, cheering the men through just before the sun sets. It then gets harder to work out who's who, but it's easy to know when Courtney Dauwalter's approaching by the wave of sound – '*Allez*! *Allez*, Courtney!' It's her third 100-miler in 10 weeks, and no one – including by her own admission Courtney herself – knows how it's going to go. I shout encouragement as she runs past, trying to make out the expression on her face. What is she feeling right now? How is she mentally approaching the 129 mountainous kilometres (80 miles) that lie ahead? How much of the 322 kilometres (200 miles) of recent racing is still making its presence felt in her body?

A little while after Courtney, we cheer again as we spot Jo Meek running through. I've known of Jo for as long as I've been running and, now in her late 40s, she's as strong as ever, finishing high up in many of the biggest ultras on the British and international scene.

We watch the race unfold on the livestream, marvelling at the incredible level of support and enthusiasm for the runners. In places, it could be the final stretch of the climb up Alpe D'Huez in the Tour de France rather than this niche sport of mountain ultrarunning. Courtney struggles at times to find her way through the wall of cheering fans. Posters and banners with her name on line the route. Coloured smoke flares fill the air. At one point, there's so much smoke she has to slow down and take off her glasses to wipe her eyes. I watch with awe at this celebration and recognition of one remarkable woman's achievement this year and simultaneous discomfort at the closeness of the crowds, the grabbing and touching, the mass of sound and physicality that this rabble represents. I wonder how Courtney feels in that moment; sleep deprived, mountain weary, one slender figure amid such force. Later on, the camera follows her down the final descent towards the finish in Chamonix, a teenage girl running beside her, encouraged by her, shielded by her. For a long time, it looks like it's just the two of them, until the camera pans round to show a vast crowd of runners behind, all riding the wave of Courtney's now-certain victory. In the interviews that follow the race she is measured, voicing her appreciation for the support alongside and her surprise at how crazy it all was.

In the men's race, USA athletes Jim Walmsley and Zach Miller battle it out to be the first across the finish line. The commentary repeatedly claims the two men are racing to be the first American to win the coveted UTMB title; but, as Jim points out after he crosses the finish line victorious and is asked how it feels: 'I'm happy to add my name to the list of American women who have already won here. I'm proud to stand on their shoulders.'

Jim is inspiring this year for more reasons than his fabulous finishing quote. One of the most successful ultrarunners of all time, he made the switch to the mountains a few years ago and it's his fifth attempt at UTMB. After finishing fifth in 2017, he failed to finish in 2018 and 2021 and then, in 2022, having moved to the Alps with the sole aim of preparing for the race, he finished fourth, fading after a strong run in the first half. He could so easily have given up, but instead he faced the possibility of yet another failure – even dedicating his life to the cause by leaving friends and family behind and moving here, with his wife Jess, to train in the right environment.

* * *

We're back in the quiet mountains of the Beaufortain, a couple of valleys and a world away from Chamonix. It's a year since I was last here, which means it's also a year since I first took on this challenge to learn how to run 100 miles. Back then, I had no idea that I still wouldn't have achieved this goal a year on. That I'd still be searching for all the ingredients that would, if I was lucky, come together on a specific day to create the conditions to succeed.

Running in the mountains this time around, though, I know I'm a long way on from where I was last year. I am stronger, braver, happier and wiser in my running. I can think back over 12 months of consistent training and good, long, hilly and often mountainous training, too. Sim and I find we cannot run every day here; it becomes too much of a fight against fatigue. Instead, we run every other day, spending three, four or five hours out on the mountain trails. As I run without the disabling fear of the past, it feels as though I am both finding and forging my way.

Every evening my belly groans, overfull with the amount of food and water it takes to fuel these adventures. I find the constant hunger and need to eat almost more tiring than the running. My ankle is still swollen but that doesn't seem to hinder my running. I work hard at keeping it moving, maintaining mobility, balance and strength, trying to limit its effect on both the area local to the ankle and my wider biomechanics. But I am addicted to these high-up days. I fall in love with the alpine pastures; stripy, fluffy marmots that flow over rocks or stand high on outcrops, watchful, still as statues; the gentle, honey-coloured cows with their giant bells that fill the hills with music; the wolves I know are in the forests but that I thankfully never see; the huge grasshoppers with red and blue underwings; the soaring buzzards, eagles, kestrels and once even a bearded vulture; the bright-yellow swallowtail butterfly I've been looking for since I was nine.

Last year, Sim had made an ascent of the highest mountain in the local range: Grand Mont, at 2,686 metres (8,812 feet). I'd been in awe back then, thinking I'd never do that – at least not on my own. But this year it's my secret goal – so secret I've not even fully admitted it to myself. Outwardly, I've been telling myself and Sim that, if everything comes together, I'll at least go and have a look.

On Big Mountain Day I set out a little later than I'd planned. There's rain forecast, turning to snow higher up, but not until this evening. I think I have enough time to get to the top and back as I set off up the long climb – around three hours from door to summit – but I keep half an eye on the sky, watching for the clouds to see how fast they're coming in, how dark they're looking. Still, I refuse to put pressure on myself, repeating that I can turn around at any point, that however far I get will be an achievement and further than I managed last time.

It's an alluringly direct line from the apartment to the summit; almost the shortest route between A and B. The lower slopes are familiar – leg-sappingly, lung-crushingly steep, the path zigzagging up a piste put to grass and cattle for the summer, the wires of the ski lift burring overhead. I pass the first ski-lift station, suspended in out-of-season silence, and push on to the wide sweep of grass that corners to the next plateau. Here, alpine meadow thrives and bilberry bushes, reddening with the first hints of autumn, cloak the mountainsides with fire. Curious cows watch me as I walk past – ultrarunning vet Emma Stuart says never to run past cows. I look into their liquid brown eyes, feeling the rise of my heart rate and the flood of adrenaline even though I'm fairly sure they're not going to chase me. They're just huge and there are a lot of them. I like cows but, like dogs, I never fully trust them. I love how the views open out as I climb higher – unfolding mountain after mountain after mountain in every direction. I look down into the village, now tiny and far below, and try to spot the roof of our apartment building. In the far distance, the bright-white summit of Mont Blanc shimmers in the sun.

I soon reach the highest point I've been on this mountain and from here on it's all new – terrifyingly, exhilaratingly so. For a while, the terrain's similar: ski infrastructure, pistes and tracks taking the path of least resistance through the rocky mountain terrain. But, after the top ski lift, everything suddenly becomes wilder. I feel like I'm crossing into a realm that's not just an unknown for me, but an altogether less-visited place.

Grand Mont isn't particularly difficult to climb, but it's high and remote and a long walk from anywhere. The only technically challenging terrain lies in this top section, which requires scrambling up through a boulder field before eventually gaining the summit.

I pause for a few moments before committing, letting my breathing settle after the climb, drinking some water, eating some of the cake I've brought. The abrupt summit ridge rises directly ahead, but my route traverses around to the left – taking a longer but gentler option, which also has the way marked in sporadic splashes of yellow paint on the rocks. The dark clouds I spotted in the distance from lower down are now spreading, filling up the skyline beyond the top of the mountain. I need to make a decision quickly. If I'm going to continue, at least to a point where I can see the summit, I don't have a lot of time before those clouds close in and drop whatever they're holding. I'm feeling good, and I've got plenty of food, water and protective clothing with me. I decide I'm going to go for it.

The landscape changes completely as I step onto the moonscape of boulders that tumbles from the summit, still high above and well out of my sight. The rock is a uniform pale grey, grippy underfoot. Small, glassy lakes have formed here and there in shallow depressions. I dip a hand into one, feeling the ache of its cold. For the most part, the yellow paint splashes make the way up easy to follow – there's no path here, no obvious way worn into the stones. Sometimes I can't immediately spot the next mark and anxiety pinches at me – what if I've gone the wrong way and end up lost or on dangerous ground? But I have a map, which I check each time I'm unsure; and each time it's a gentle reminder that I am competent and this is something I can do.

After what feels like a long time climbing, the gradient eases and suddenly the summit appears ahead. It's only a little higher than I am, but I need to climb down through a shallow, snow-filled gully and then back up to the summit proper. The snow's slippery in places, but I'm careful and take my time. It's a fight against the excitement and impatience about reaching the top. *Don't mess up now.*

The moment I reach the big wooden cross that marks the summit of Grand Mont, my phone rings. It's Sim. He's been watching my dot on the tracking app we use when we're running in places like this and he wants to congratulate me on getting there. He's genuinely happy for me – he knows it will have been a big deal, but he'd never have let on that he knew that before I left. He's always absolutely encouraging, completely believing in my abilities to do the things I want to do. I hope I do the same for him, and our children.

I want to spend a long time at the summit, simply drinking in the rows and rows of jagged mountains in every direction. But those dark clouds are descending now and the view is starting to disappear. I descend to the snowy gully, out of the wind, and put on extra layers of clothes, eat and drink and check the map for my descent path. After the thrill of a summit success, it's so easy to get it wrong on the way down.

The weather chases me as I descend and I feel I'm running just at the edge of the storm. I just make it home before the first rain falls. The following morning, the higher peaks are covered with snow. I couldn't have left it another day.

My Grand Mont adventure takes me just shy of five hours, covering an unimpressive-sounding 19.6 kilometres (12 miles) and a slightly more credible 1,785 metres (5,856 feet) of ascent. But it's up there with the things I'm most proud of. I could easily have quit and turned back so many times on my way up. With snow on the ground and more snow forecast, it wasn't always clear that carrying on was the right choice. But I'd used my judgement, managed my energy reserves, known I had the fitness, skills and equipment to deal with most eventualities and had made it to the top and back safely. I'd still had the unhelpful niggling voice reminding me of the dangers of cows, angry shepherd dogs, guns, wolves, strange men and freak rockfall. By other people's standards it was perhaps just a normal day out in the mountains; but for me it was huge and the sense of satisfaction lingers – in fact, it's still with me now.

* * *

A few days after we return to the UK, Sim is due to run a 177-kilometre (110-mile) race along the north coast of Devon. It's been planned for a long time, and for much of this time he's thought he might postpone his entry to next year. But we've had a good block of training in the Alps, with long days on our feet, lots of climbs and descents, and the adaptations that occur with training at altitude. When he entered the race we both assumed I'd have long since run my own 100-miler. But now that it's fast approaching and I'm not going to have done so, Sim is concerned.

'Do you mind if I run it?' he asks, testing the water – knowing I'd never stop him, but also knowing that it must be a strange feeling for me, having tried and failed at several attempts at my own challenge.

Of course I don't mind. There isn't a single part of me that resents his taking on his own 100-miler. I'm only proud, and supportive, and impressed that he's keen to give it a go. I also have no doubt that he'll do it. I know how tough he is physically, how well suited he is to it psychologically and how he'll meticulously plan every element to give himself the very best chance of success on the day.

There's a narrative that's often trotted out, which says that women over-prepare while men are happy to wing it. But, like all unhelpful stereotypes, this is of course nonsense in most cases and a lazy assessment of a few. Sim is organized, considered and utterly committed to being as prepared as he can be when he takes on big challenges. He's fully aware of the cost – in terms of both time and money – that doing races like this places on the rest of us. He's all but put aside his plans to run this race, but as everything has gone perfectly there's no reason why he shouldn't.

We make the long trip home from France, feeling like we've left part of our souls high in the mountains and promising our yearning selves that we'll be back. In the few days before Sim's race, no one comes down with a cold and there are no sprained ankles or freak thunderstorms. Everyone sleeps perfectly. The weather is forecast to be dry and sunny, with highs of 20°C degrees and lows of 13°C (68°F and 54.5°F) – weird for October but about as perfect as it gets for ultrarunning.

Sim's race is early on Friday morning and he's planning to sleep in the car somewhere near the start. On Thursday evening I hug him tight and wish him luck, then watch him drive off into the darkness. I lock the door and sob silently to myself for a few moments, standing in the hallway, not wanting the kids to see. It's a complicated wave of emotion that takes me by surprise. A mixture of normal concern for a loved one setting out on a pretty big and gnarly challenge; and then the fact that we'll all miss him – he's our rock and ever present in our daily lives. There's also the rawness of leaving the mountains so recently and our big, summer-long adventure having come to an end; and then there's just how hard getting to this point – the start of a race, let alone much further – has been for me over the past months. I'm crying not through envy that Sim's race seems to be coming together – because there's nothing I want more at this moment than for him to have a fantastic race – but in lament for all my own failed attempts.

First thing on Friday morning, after a brief pre-race

phone call with Sim, I sit with Hugo to do his reading, as we do at this time every day.

'Guess what,' I say to him. 'Tomorrow morning, when we next do your reading, Daddy will *still* be running.'

He looks at me with big eyes, almost uncomprehending the scale of this amount of time. 'Wow.'

For the whole of Friday, I watch Sim's dot make its way along the South West Coast Path. I take a few breaks from this mission, of course – to write, make food for the kids, take the dog for a walk and even do a quick run on the treadmill – but the dot-checking is impulsive and compulsive. I'm clearly not the only one. My phone pings regularly with comments from our family and friends, also finding themselves preoccupied by the dot. It's an interesting insight into their existence while I'm running.

I wake up three or four times in the night to check Sim's tracker and send him encouraging messages; and it's the first thing I do when I wake up in the morning. It's such a different experience, being the watcher, the waiter, the one at home. I think that sense of helplessness – the disconnectedness of being so far away and removed from the experience – is in some ways as hard as being out there in the middle of it. Only there's no control over times, paces or nutrition strategies – all that is completely out of my hands. My job is to keep everything together at home; to make sure the kids are happy and healthy and the work and washing up get done. It's a different kind of endurance, and quitting isn't an option.

Sim finishes fifth man and sixth overall, with three women finishing in the top ten. It's been a tough couple of days out for them, with unseasonably warm temperatures, high humidity, covering the long distance and around 6,000 metres (19,685 feet) of ascent along the way. I'm really happy for Sim – and incredibly proud. But, as I listen to him talk about his experiences – those that might have stopped some people but through which he pushed on – I realize he's now joined that elusive club I've been longing to be a member of for so long. By persevering, he knows how it feels to have crossed the finish line of a 100-miler. He's had that transformative experience so many people I've spoken to have told me about. You're never the same again once you've crossed that finish line, they said. He'll never be the same again.

I listen with intense fascination to his stories of hallucinations – the cracks in the rocks that became hundreds of lizards as he passed, the tree branches that morphed into animals, the garden ornament that he was convinced was a real little old man sitting on a wall. I'm impressed by his self-management, how he'd avoided tipping too far by taking in salt, sugar and fluid. He ran a measured race, prioritizing self-preservation over competition, taking a 20-minute nap even though he wasn't that tired. He has sore feet, blisters on top of blisters and one under his big toenail that almost certainly means the nail will fall off, and I know he'll struggle with the stairs for a few days to come, but these are the war wounds of a successful mission and the pain is borne with well-earned pride.

In finishing his 100-miler, Sim has crossed to the other side of something that for me has so far been insurmountable; he has accessed a place I'm not privy to. I don't begrudge him that in the slightest – in fact I find him irresistible, amusing myself with how proud I am of my hero having returned from battle – but I have to acknowledge that there's a frustration and melancholy behind my joy for his achievement. He succeeded where I failed. He pushed on where I quit. All it took was to simply keep going, one foot in front of the other, and he had understood this at that crucial point where I had let it go.

I remember feeling something similar during the first weeks after finishing our prenatal classes, when those of our group who'd had the earliest due dates arrived with their babies. I looked at those women I'd got to know before they became mothers. Now they'd been through something that had fundamentally changed them – an experience that I could not yet even begin to comprehend. But, as my burgeoning belly constantly reminded me, it wouldn't be long before I would also pass through that transitional time; until I, too, showed up altered, with a brand-new being in my arms. While things could go wrong, me choosing to quit wasn't going to be one of them. This time, though, it's all up to me. Do I have what it takes, or not?

I struggle with the selfishness and self-centredness of these thoughts, but I can't entirely distance myself from them. In the first couple of days after Sim's race, half of me wants to

243

hug him and celebrate him while the other half wants to collapse onto the floor in despair over my uselessness. I've always known that the only way I can answer the question of whether or not I'm someone who can run 100 miles is to keep trying. Now, the question is right up against me: can I do it? I'm pretty sure my body can make it, but is my mind capable of hanging on in there for the ride?

* * *

Two opportunities to try to run 100 miles pass during the months after our return from France. First, the Autumn 100, a race I'm told is a perfect first 100 as it's organized by highly experienced race organizers Centurion Running and consists of 4 x 40-kilometre (25-mile) out-and-back legs that form a cross-shaped route. After each leg, runners return to a central base, where their drop bag and Centurion's famous hospitality await.

When I enter this race, I don't feel inspired by the course – in fact my fear of running through Reading in the middle of the night eclipses most other thoughts about it – but I'm comforted by the fact that several of the women I've spoken to reported good things about it. However, as the date to withdraw my entry approaches, and my ankle continues to hurt with every run – including an ominous sharp pain along the narrow fibula bone on the outside of the ankle – I fret about the wisdom of trying to do it. I've lost a lot of movement in the ankle joint, too, and it still swells noticeably after longer runs.

I focus on rehabilitating the ankle as much as I

can – standing one-legged on an inflatable wobble cushion several times a day, working on mobility and strengthening exercises – but progress is irritatingly slow. When I feel the lower part of the fibula, pressing along the bone with my fingers, the sharp pain extends right across the narrowest part, just above the bony bulge of the lateral malleolus – the prominence on the outside of the ankle. I think it likely that I badly stressed the bone when I landed on it; perhaps I even managed a small fracture. It is all stable, and will heal in time, but running 100 miles with it like this risks a full fracture and potentially much longer-term damage. And, of course, failing to finish another race.

On the last day possible, with my ankle still nowhere near better, I click on the cancel button to request a refund of my entry fee. I will not be running the Autumn 100. Scrolling through the few remaining ultras scheduled for the coming winter, I come across two possibilities. The first is the appropriately named Full Circle, which takes in a complete circumnavigation of Dartmoor in November. That sounds perfect – Sim and the kids could stay at his parents' house, not far from the start, while I ran through a landscape I love and in which I feel both safe and inspired. And I'd get my 100-miler done before Christmas, which feels like a nice aim.

The other possibility is a race I've followed for years but have never considered entering – the terrifyingly named Arc of Attrition, which takes in 100 miles of the South West Coast Path around the westernmost edge of Cornwall in

January. Organized by MudCrew and, from 2025 onwards part of UTMB's world series, it's become one of the UK's top winter ultras, drawing many big names and with a list of winners that includes Anna Troup, Nicky Spinks and Emma Stuart.

The Arc has been full for months, but I add myself to the waiting list just in case. I am learning that nothing's a given when it comes to getting to the start line, let alone the finish line, of 100-mile races. Then I enter the Full Circle, download the route onto my OS Maps app and start planning. Even the name 'Full Circle' feels wonderfully apt. After all these months of trying and failing to run 100 miles, I would finally be coming full circle and completing my goal in a place I thought of as my second home.

In the end, though, this plan – like so many others over the past few years – is thwarted by illness and I don't even get to the start line. Despondency starts to set in. Perhaps I'll never reach my 100-mile goal.

But the (Arc) Angels are on my side. With less than two months to go until the start of the Arc of Attrition, I receive an email. I've got a place: 100 miles is on once again.

13

ARC OF ATTRITION

'The best thing about 100 miles is that your job is to put one foot in front of the other and to eat. And as a mum of two when do you get to have that kind of day? How freaking cool is that? One foot in front of the other and eat your sandwiches.'

—Lucy Bartholomew, multiple
race winner

In my early twenties, I moved from a Midlands city that made me unhappy to an utterly picturesque village on the South Devon coast. At that point, it was the best major life decision I'd ever made. I still vividly remember the exhilarating sense of freedom the move gave me. I'd leave my tiny, rented flat and within minutes would be running along the edge of the harbour, surrounded by the soothing music of jingling boats and the rhythmic wash of the waves. Ever since that move, the sea has been a source of calm and respite. If I'm feeling restless, watching the endlessly restless sea is the cure.

Later, during a period when we'd called a 4-metre bell

tent home, the south coasts of both Devon and Cornwall were our winter refuge. Over the coldest, darkest months we found warmth there; in the sheltered sandy coves and closeknit communities who rediscover themselves anew when the tourists leave. The sea, and that stretch of coastline, are what I need right now.

This winter, we've already had a bad cold that took me out of training for two weeks. Friends with families came down with COVID, norovirus and flu. Since becoming a mum, training over the winter months has always been filled with uncertainty. With no race to train for this doesn't matter so much; but with my final attempt at a 100-miler before my book deadline fast approaching, I need to do everything I can to control the controllables.

I find an annex to a house in Mullion, on the Lizard Peninsula, that looks like it might just about be within our budget for the two weeks running up to the Arc. It feels a little excessive, but I'm desperate. We'll be able to work from the house and the kids will get to spend two weeks by the sea, on the beaches, getting to know Cornwall. One of the couple who owns the house is also a trail runner and knows all about the Arc. His friend Mel finished it last year and he kindly puts us in touch. After a few emails, Mel and I arrange to meet on a local beach with all our kids in tow – like me, she has two, and they're all a similar age.

I see them in the distance, making their way over the dunes. Mel is easy to spot – the embodiment of a runner, she's wearing Hoka trainers, running tights and a La

Sportiva Arc of Attrition down jacket that I covet. She's got long, red hair and shades. She's cool, I think, as we introduce ourselves and the kids.

The Arc was Mel's first 100-mile race and I get the feeling she wants to do it again. We spend a couple of hours talking about running, ultrarunning and specifically the Arc, drinking hot chocolate while the kids play on the beach like they've been friends for years. As a dazzling sunset lights up the sea and sky, we start to shiver and run down the beach to retrieve them. Mel is encouraging but also practical in her words.

'Have the soup!' she says. 'I left every checkpoint with a mug of soup – it was great.' She also recommends recceing the final mile of the course, which takes in the biggest single climb of the entire route at Porthtowan.

I feel calmer after speaking with Mel. Her race hadn't gone to plan – she'd walked a lot more of it than she'd intended to – but she'd just refused to give up. That's all I need to do.

It's Sunday morning – the day before the start of Arc week. This time on Friday I'll be trying to force down porridge and double, triple, quadruple checking I've got everything I should have in my race pack. I wonder if I'll manage to sleep the night before. Perhaps I should try to get some help for my sleeping problems. Too late now, for this race at least. I'll just have to do my best. I've had a headache, a sore throat and blocked nose for the past few days. I've been wondering whether it's all psychosomatic – after all, we've been in quarantine for the past two weeks – but Hugo is complaining of something similar. It doesn't seem to be getting any worse, so I try not to add it to my list of things to worry about.

The days are dragging horribly. After my overenthusiastic recces last week, my right knee developed a slight twinge when I bent it. I'd decided to play it safe; after all, the last couple of weeks before a big race are supposed to be a taper – a wind-down to allow the body to heal and strengthen ready for the race. Taper tantrums are notorious in running and particularly in ultrarunning, when habitual high mileage, emotional dependence on running and the need for a longer than average taper all converge to create a kind of inner hell. For my part, after four days of gentle walks, trying to avoid the steep steps and rocky terrain of the coast path, I feel like I've never run before. Then a big storm blows in, with 97kph (60mph) winds careering unhindered off the nearby sea, firing angry rain at the windows and thumping the letterbox in a way that sends the dog skittering under the table. Caged in, I do what I can, but I realize (with a twinge of guilt at the privilege and self-centredness of it) how empty life feels without running. I keep eating, but food doesn't taste as good or satisfy like it does after a run. I work, but even my thoughts seem sludgy. I'm sinking into a stasis-inspired torpor thinking if I never try to run 100 miles again, it'll be to avoid the need to taper.

* * *

There's a dense crowd of bodies at the start of the Arc of Attrition 2024. Music throbs. Nervous chatter swells.

The queue for the men's toilets stretches across the car park. In the ladies' we celebrate that there is a queue at all – there never would have been at a race of this distance just a few years ago.

Sim's at the start taking photos and I feel torn between focusing on him or my impending departure. Part of me longs to run away from the people and the noise, back to the cottage with him and the kids – to join the party they have planned for the evening while I'm out running. But another part yearns for the adventure, the self-reliance, the pain of what is to come.

We'd driven to Porthtowan the previous evening so I could register. I'd felt excited but calm then; happy to be among so many other people that shared the same love. That sense of belonging that I've felt grow as I've increasingly immersed myself in this world was stronger than ever. It felt like I'd found my place. I'd also been allocated race number 22 – which seemed like an unbelievable stroke of luck for someone born on 22/02 at 22:22. I'd bumped into Kirsty Reade, too, who was also there registering, and we'd chatted about the route, the weather, books and women in ultrarunning.

'How's training been?' she'd asked as we conversed at a shout over the music and chatter.

'Not too bad . . . I think.' Looking back now that it's too late to do anything about it, I'm not really sure. Long-term, over the past year and more, I've done some of the most consistent, most adventurous running of my life; but over the past weeks that's been much less the case.

'We managed to get a nasty cold in November and then COVID at Christmas,' I said. 'Other than that . . . okay.'

Kirsty had told me about missing out on her training race – the 64-kilometre (40-mile) Tour de Helvellyn – due to illness and worried that she hasn't run a 100 since the summer. Then she realized what she'd said, remembering what a big deal this distance is for me and that I've *never* run 100 miles before.

'Sorry – I probably sound like a total arsehole saying that, don't I?!' We laughed. Kirsty couldn't sound like an arsehole if she tried.

Music builds and runners push towards the start. I put my earphones in. Not to listen to anything, but just to remove some of the noise. It's all too much otherwise – my nervous energy combined with that of everyone around me, the crowds, the harshness of sounds, the smells, even the brightness of the midday light.

A countdown begins: three minutes to go. I make my way forward but not too far forward; I don't want to be anywhere near the front. I keep to the side – my favourite spot, on the edge of things, where it's easy to escape.

Two minutes to go.

I spot Sim standing on a wall nearby, camera poised.

'Smile!' He aims the lens at me.

Jokingly, I bring my hands to my face, pretending to chew my nails with nerves. He snaps a picture. It's one of my favourites from the day.

The crowd moves in further, funnelled into a too-small gap by the start gantry. The air is heavy with the closeness of bodies now – nervous bodies – the farts and breath and sweat and lube.

One minute to go.

We jostle forward again. A man just in front of me stumbles and steps back, right onto my toe. He apologizes quickly. 'Ah well – I can't do it now!' I say, and we laugh. It breaks the tension just a little. I remember to breathe. Focusing on the feeling of air filling my body and leaving it again. Breathe in, breathe out. I battle to stay anchored while the chords of Led Zepplin's 'Kashmir' build into the final countdown.

Five . . . Four . . . Three . . . Two . . . One . . .

And then it's happening. I'm running a 100-mile race. Not ill, not injured, not cancelled, not fretting with worry about the kids, just running, in the sunshine, with nearly 400 other runners. Together, we round the corner in Coverack, the smoke from flares billowing all around. Through the haze, the sun glints on a bright-blue sea. Yesterday brought strong winds and rain. The forecast is similar for Saturday evening, around race cutoff time. But right now, for January, for these two days and a night, it couldn't be more perfect.

Sometimes, I think, feeling a grin spreading across my face, very occasionally, it does all come together.

The road out of Coverack climbs steeply up and around a corner, a hill I'd usually walk in any long run. But I keep the pace up, remembering what others have said about the bottlenecks that happen a little further on where the path narrows. Thinking the start would be slow, I haven't warmed up, and my legs and lungs burn with effort. I'm working far harder than I should be this early on in the race.

We soon reach the narrow paths, scurrying between hostile blackthorn, all bare winter prickles with no chance of overtaking. We slow to a walk, sometimes a halt. No one seems to mind. The coastline stretches away into the distance – all those miles yet to run, tracing the edge of the land towards its westernmost point. And then the same again on the other side, as yet out of sight.

Having run this stretch of the path a week or so ago, on a sunny day like this one, I've brought my sunglasses and I'm grateful for their shade. We set out at noon and the winter sun lowers as we run west, straight into its glare.

With the overexcitement of the start and first few miles behind me, I realize how terrible I feel. The headache, sore throat and general achiness that have been hanging around for the past few days set in, amplified by the initial exertion. My first thought is that this seems a bit unfair, given how much I've tried to avoid getting ill. But then I realize that while it might not be perfect, it's not that bad. I'm still running, the finish still feels possible: accept that this is how it's going to be and move on. For the moment at least, it's not affecting my running except by taking away a bit of the enjoyment.

We make our way around the Lizard Peninsula, a place that's come to feel a little like home over the past weeks. The tightly packed line of runners gradually spreads out as we emerge from the confines of the path onto coastal grassland. At Lizard Point, a crowd of crews await their runners, cheering the rest of us through. I don't have crew, so I just carry on through the sudden noise and buzz and then back into the peace and the race again.

There are some exposed sections of the coast path here, where the trail clings to the edge of the land and one stumble in the wrong direction could pitch you over the edge into the roaring sea. I've spent so much time on this trail, so much time on cliffs that feel like they're at the very edge of the world, that I've learned to ignore these precipitous drops and the possible but unlikely consequences of a fall. I'm traversing one of these sections, enjoying the gentle thrill of the position, when a petite blonde woman ahead of me stops suddenly.

'Shit the bed!' she says, taking me utterly by surprise.

I ask her if she's okay and she explains she gets terrible vertigo, but that she'll be fine. I do my best to help, suggesting trying to focus on the trail beneath and a little way in front of her feet, pretending the yawning, heaving gulf simply doesn't exist. It's always worked for me.

It's her first time at the Arc, too. She seems like a strong runner, skipping off into the distance on the flatter sections, but is clearly struggling with the technical, exposed trail. I realize that the extent to which everyone is battling isn't necessarily obvious to those outside their immediate lived experience – we all bring our personal demons with us to these challenges.

I've arranged to meet Sim and the kids at Mullion, about 29 kilometres (18 miles) in. It's the only place I'll see them on the route and I'm looking forward to it, but as I approach I realize we haven't agreed exactly where to meet. My headache's worsening and I've started feeling sick – in fact, I feel oddly hungover. There's no sign of my family as I run through the main crew point in Mullion and I feel a little mournful as I pass other runners being cared for by their crew.

I pass the next point at which we could have met, but they're not there either. I try ringing Sim but it goes straight through to his answerphone. Anxiety starts to niggle. What if something's happened? Why wouldn't they be here but not let me know? I stand still for a moment, unsure what to do. But the only thing I can do is carry on, so I descend the giant steps we've walked up and down so many times since we arrived in Cornwall, heading to the beach at Polurrian. And there they are, of course, waiting for me with massive smiles, the dog barking and wagging his tail crazily. The kids tell me about the sharks' eggs they've found on the beach.

I hug them all and take orange juice and paracetamol from the stash of offerings they've brought. I don't fancy much else. Then we say goodbye and the kids run back to the beach without so much as a backward glance. It's wonderful to see them so happy, so carefree. But as I climb the steep path on the opposite side of the bay, up to the next headland, I look down on them and find my vision blurry with tears. Made tiny now by distance, oblivious of my gaze, right there – *right there* – are the most important things in my life . . . and I'm running away from them. Sim must sense my gaze because he turns and lifts a hand to wave and I blow him a kiss, sending it out from the cliffs to the figures on the sand far below. The sun is sinking now and it will soon be getting dark. There's a yearning – a deep, lonely ache in my chest – because I know this will be the first night I've spent away from my children. But I can't stay. I have a job to do.

Goodnight, my loves. See you tomorrow.

We're treated to a glorious sunset – a blaze of gold spreading into orange and red against a pale-blue evening sky and a deep blue sea. Watching the last glimmering speck of fire vanish below the waves, I turn to another runner.

'We're so lucky to get a sunset!'

She agrees and we fall into step, running together in silence for a while, taking in the beauty of the sky and sea from our high trail across the headland. Eventually, we descend onto the beach at Loe Bar as dusk is rolling in, inking the edges of our worlds. We decide we should have just enough light to get to the first checkpoint in Porthcurno before we need to get our headtorches out.

It's pleasant jogging across the shingle, the swell of the sea to one side and the flat calm of Loe Pool to the other, chatting about motherhood, work and the escapism and adventure of ultrarunning. She's run five 100-milers but finishing is still far from guaranteed, she tells me. She struggles with some long-term health problems for which she has to take medication with unpleasant side effects; and she had to drop out of a recent 100-mile race as she felt so ill. I'm still battling with my headache and nausea, but it suddenly doesn't feel quite so bad.

'People assume that because I've done a few already I somehow find it easier,' she says. 'But each time it's like starting again, because you never know with these longer races.'

One of the many special things about the Arc of Attrition is its volunteers: the Arc Angels. As we arrive in Porthleven at 40 kilometres (25 miles), where the first checkpoint awaits us, we're greeted by a line of runners clad in high-vis jackets. These incredible humans run with us to the checkpoint, show us the way in, ask if we need any medical attention and check we're fine before heading back out to collect the next runner. It's something I've never come across before in a race and it's wonderful.

At the checkpoint I'm overwhelmed by the lights and noise and smell of food, which hit me the moment I step inside. I'm desperate for a pee – I have been for a while but there's been nowhere to go – so I take care of that first and then, remembering what Mel told me, get myself a cup of hot soup. There are runners everywhere, mostly sitting down, eating food off plates. But I can't think straight, so I head straight back out, soup in hand. It's only when I get outside that I realize I still haven't put my headtorch on and it is now completely dark. I spend far too long trying to balance the soup on the uneven ground, giving up and holding the lip of the cup between my teeth, unzipping my bag, arranging my torch on my head and eventually setting out again, trying not to pour the soup everywhere as I jog along. Perhaps this hadn't been the greatest idea – I'd have been quicker and more effective sitting down and sorting myself out. I make a mental note to do that next time, which will be Penzance, 24 kilometres (15 miles) away.

For so long, running in the dark was one of the things I found most frightening about the prospect of undertaking a 100-miler. But now, having recognized this fear and practised a little during the dark winter nights, I'm here in a race where I'll be running for 15 hours or more in darkness and am delighted to discover it doesn't bother me in the slightest. My headtorch is bright – more than bright enough for me to easily see where I'm running. I keep it on its medium setting, turning onto low when I'm in towns and villages with street lighting, and up to high occasionally when the ground gets technical.

I run with another woman for a little way, passing Praa Sands and beautiful, atmospheric Prussia Cove, now hidden from view in the blackness. A group of runners catches us up and I decide I'll try to stay with them. It's easy to drift on my own, losing myself in my thoughts and the soft darkness of the night. But if I can stick with the group I can cover some ground more quickly. We jog along for what feels like a few miles, just a little faster than is comfortable. Perhaps I can keep going until Penzance, I think. Then I can sit down and have a rest. Having felt a little better after the soup, I soon start to feel sick again. Then dizzy. I slow to a walk and watch the line of headtorches weave their way off into the distance.

I'm on my own, feeling terrible, when I reach the long stretch of road that traces the edge of the sea through Marazion and Penzance. I should be running faster here, making the most of the easy, flat terrain, but I can't. The moment I break into a jog I start retching, which turns into violent, painful hiccups. I walk miserably, hiccupping loudly into the night. After several attempts, I'm reduced to groaning and trying to drink water from my soft flask upside down to get rid of the dreaded things before I give up and resign myself to walking. It's a grim realization for my longed-for 100-mile finish: I'm 56 kilometres (35 miles) in and already I can't run.

The air temperature has plummeted and my breath comes out in clouds of vapour that reflect the light from my headtorch back at me. I have to switch off its energy-saving reactive mode, because this reflection makes it dim itself every time I breathe out as it assumes I'm near to an object and therefore don't need to be able to see very far ahead.

'Jen Benson number 22!' A voice shakes me from my rumination. It's Kirsty, who probably stopped for a little longer at Porthleven, ran a more measured pace from there and has now caught me up. I explain my problem to her – that I can walk but as soon as I run it makes me sick and gives me hiccups. She sympathizes – she's not feeling great herself. She offers me various things, but each suggestion makes my mouth water and not in a good way. I tell her I'll be fine – I'll just keep walking.

'It will pass, you know,' she tells me, with absolute certainty, before disappearing into the distance. It's just what I need to hear and I cling onto it as the miles crawl by.

Kirsty is still at the checkpoint in Penzance at 64 kilometres (40 miles) when I arrive. She's staring into a cup of what turns out to be a thick, brown soup. I sit next to her and we exchange a few words. Then she seems to make up her mind about something.

'I can't eat this,' she says.

She wishes me well, gathers her things and leaves. Other runners come in; other runners leave. I want to change my socks because the ones I'm wearing are soaked, but being unable to run or eat has meant my body temperature has dropped and now I'm shivering so violently it takes me an age to undo my gaiters and shoes, take my socks off, apply some lube to my feet, put my dry socks back on and then reassemble my shoes and gaiters. When I look up, one of the Arc Angels is looking at me with concern.

'You're too cold,' she says. 'You can't go back out like that. Have you eaten anything?'

I explain that I'm feeling too sick to eat, but that I'll be fine once I get moving again. My forced cheerful tone doesn't wash with this Angel.

'I can't let you go back out until you've stopped shaking. I'll get a blanket – hang on.'

She goes and fetches a warm blanket, moves me to a seat out of the draught of the door and wraps me up. It's a soft, pale-blue blanket that smells of washing powder. I feel like I'm five years old and have just got out of the cold sea, with my mum wrapping me in a warm towel. Leaving me to warm up, the Angel fetches tea and watermelon. I stare at the plate of garish pink and green and realize it's the first food I've seen for a while that hasn't made my stomach turn. I take a slice and manage to eat it, then manage another two. And suddenly I'm feeling better.

'Right,' says my new favourite person in the world. 'Now let's get you some hot pizza.'

Ten minutes later, I'm warm, moving again and carrying three slices of takeaway pizza in a folded paper plate. For a few moments in the aid station, I'd wondered whether the decision to carry on was going to be taken out of my hands – that if I couldn't warm up I would be pulled from the race on safety grounds. But, thanks to an Angel and some watermelon, I'm now back on my way. Still walking, but making progress.

I wish I'd asked the Angel's name, but I was too blurry and disorientated at the time to think of doing so. I said thank you to her many times, though, and I hope she knows how grateful I am. She saved my race.

The 26 kilometres (16 miles) from Penzance to Land's End is the loneliest of the whole race. Despite feeling much better than I had before arriving at Penzance, I still can't run more than a few uncomfortable steps at a time. I can walk – and fast, striding along not much slower than running pace – but the moment I break into a run, the nausea is right back like a kick in the stomach. So, I make my slow but steady way along the South West Coast Path, up the steep hill out of Mousehole village, around the tricky, rocky, exposed section before Lamorna, past Treen and Porthcurno, where, with my six-months-pregnant belly, we'd spent our honeymoon, camping, eating wedding cake and ambling along these very trails. After Porthcurno is the steep climb up to the Minack Theatre and I haul myself up using the handrails, my arms willingly taking over some of the work from my legs for a while. Crews with their cars and vans fill the car park at the top. There's also a mobile aid station for runners without crew; and I refill my water bottle, exchange a few cheerful words and set off again with a couple of Jaffa Cakes. It's 2am and I'm so grateful to these volunteers, who seem to pop up to look after us at the moments we most need them.

The final 16 kilometres (10 miles) or so to Land's End cross some of the most remote terrain in West Cornwall. The land rises and falls steeply, like huge waves, with lesser-used trails that are often muddy and boggy in the valleys. I sink into mud deeper than my gaiters on a couple of occasions. The seas are still heavy following the recent storms and real waves roar in, thundering through the rocky caverns below, hitting the cliffs that edge mainland Britain just metres from our feet with Earth-shaking force. A nearly full wolf moon passes in and out of wispy cloud, embossing the tar-black surface of the sea with bright silver. It's at once terrifying and magnificent. I'm no longer cold, but the awesome, elemental power of it all makes me shiver.

Having been on my own for what feels like a long time, I join two other runners for the last stretch to Land's End. We can see the lights of the Land's End Hotel, a beacon of warmth and comfort shining out into our dark, muddy, sleep-deprived world, for a long time before we eventually get there. The Angels are there to meet us again and I run in with a friendly chap who asks if there's anything he can get for me. I'm still not hungry, which is strange for me as I'm usually happy to eat at any point on longer runs, but I agree to a couple of small slices of pizza and make my way through half of one as I repeat the routine of changing into clean, dry socks. My big toes usually become sore during longer runs, but I taped them both before setting out and it worked perfectly and the tape is still in place and doing its job. I look around at the runners filling the room. There's an odd juxtaposition of large, round dining tables complete with tablecloths and sick, tired, muddy people in various stages of undress, some slumped over, others taking an age to make it through a few mouthfuls of food. I chew on a corner of my pizza and return my attention to my toes. Combined eating and foot care, I realize, is something you need to get used to if you're going to run ultras.

I chat with photographer David Miller, who's hanging around at the checkpoint hoping for, in his words, some 'drama'. Allie Bailey has just left, he tells me, and I take the seat she's been sitting in, next to David. He took the photo for the cover of Allie's book about ultrarunning and addiction, *There is No Wall* – which will be published a few days after the race.

It's 4am and I'm drinking coffee and preparing to leave when a tall man in ridiculous red patterned shorts sits down on a nearby chair. He looks wrecked and sad.

'How's it going?' I ask, realizing how cheerful I sound. There's nothing like someone else clearly feeling awful to boost morale.

'I'm throwing in the towel,' he tells me. 'I can't run – every time I try to run I get terrible nausea. I've just told my crew I'm calling it a day here.'

I look at him and wonder whether he's really ready to quit. Is this really the decision he'll want to have made when he looks back on this race in a week's time? Is this the outcome he had in mind when he chose those shorts?

'I'm feeling the same,' I tell him. 'I can't run much, so I'm mainly walking. You're welcome to join me.'

He looks at me, and I can see the spark of . . . something. *This guy isn't done*, I think.

'Never quit in the chair,' I venture, drawing on all the sage advice the many ultrarunning women over the past months have bestowed upon me. 'You can always quit later. You might feel fine in a bit. You'll never know unless you try.' I decide against using Debbie Martin-Consani's 'Don't shit quit' out loud, but it's definitely a strong subtext.

I get all my stuff together, drink another coffee and prepare to leave. Then I notice red-shorts guy is looking at me.

'Would you mind if I joined you and walked for a bit?' he asks. 'Just to see if I can make it to Sennen or Cape Cornwall. I can always quit there.'

We leave the hotel together and red-shorts guy tells his crew his plan. They look delighted and give me a big double thumbs-up. It's funny, but after quitting in the Brecon Beacons just a few months ago, and with so much riding on finishing this race, stopping simply doesn't present itself as an option for me. It's hard, keeping going for hours and hours and hours, crossing rough, uneven, unpredictable terrain, managing nausea and other bodily discomforts. But not once do I consider dropping out. This is partly because my desire to finally complete my 100-mile goal is so strong it instantly eclipses any rising thoughts of stopping; partly because of the tracker on my pack – a dot on a map that I know my family and friends are watching; and partly because of the still-raw memory of the intense misery and wounding sense of failure that engulfed me after the Beacons Way.

I recall Eleanor Robinson's earnest, kind, honest words in her final email before the race:

Before you start, decide what you actually want to get out of this event. It's daunting and difficult. You probably won't enjoy the run. I'm afraid it will hurt, and you will want to give up, but if you do you will regret it and you will want to have another go. You will not want to be defeated. And, if you achieve it – if you finish – it's magic.

Over the past months and months of training, trying and never quite reaching that longed-for 100-mile finish line, I'm ready for that magic.

Red-shorts guy also has a crew to consider in his decision and its consequences. I remember the awful 2am drive of shame with my crew in Wales back in the summer. The guilt I felt that I'd let them down, that they'd put themselves out so much and I'd simply stepped away when things got a little bit tough. When you have a crew, your success is also their success. But your failure is also theirs. If I can save this man and his crew from that, I'll have salvaged a positive from my previous negative experience and achieved something beyond my own race.

Within minutes of setting off again, red-shorts guy (whose name turns out to be Dave) is chatting away happily. The next section is billed as the longest and toughest of the race, turning the westernmost corner of Cornwall and making its way up the wild and rugged north coast. We were warned in our pre-race briefing that this stretch will take longer than we expect; and that places where crew can meet us are few and far between. Dave's concerned about making the cutoff at St Ives, which is known to be tight. But, having run this section less than three weeks ago, I'm unshakeably confident. I don't think it's too bad and I offer reassurance.

We're walking, but we're hardly slower than the runners around us now, striding out with renewed purpose.

It's the early hours of the morning – perhaps three hours before daylight – but I haven't yet felt sleepy once. People have told me the last hours before dawn are the hardest for staying awake and alert, but I'm grateful that I don't experience that at all this time. I realize there are so many things I've worried about in advance of this race. I've made so many predictions about how it'll feel, how I'll manage the expected and what-if plans I can draw upon in case the unexpected happens. But it turns out I couldn't have even begun predicting the reality of the experience. The lived, conscious reality of moving so far, for so long, as night follows day and day follows night and night follows day again. Simply accepting what's thrown at us, or what we're thrown into: the weather, the mud and rocks, the physical sensations, the interactions with others, the whole evolving, unfolding, emerging, dynamic experience of this race. It's at once much huger than I'd imagined and more manageable. It's so big, I can't grasp it in its entirety. It really is one step – currently one walking step – at a time; but each of those steps is infinitely doable and it's patience, not power, that will get us to the finish.

The big black sea rolls in to our left, incessant, obsessive, relentless in its assault of the land. It's 6am. Stars speckle a clear night sky. I wonder if I can detect the tiniest amount of paler light at the eastern rim of the horizon, but it's only the moon – still huge and silver but slowly slipping below the land now. The world remains absolutely, resolutely dark almost until the very last minute. And then suddenly we find ourselves running through a soft, grey dawn.

Weaving through the mineworks at Kenidjack and Levant, the Cornish mining landscape emerging with the growing light, we fall into step with Allie Bailey. She's running the Arc for the third time, having dropped out on her first attempt and finished on her second, last year. She asks how I'm doing and I tell her about the nausea, that I've never experienced anything like this before, but that I'm loving the race. She's generous with her advice, sharing her wisdom from running more than 60 100-milers and many other ultras. She's also struggling, having picked up a foot injury, but her determination to finish is clear. I ask about her book and she starts to tell me about it; but then we're interrupted by another runner who's interested in Allie's story and we drift apart, our races separating once again.

Penwith – the westernmost peninsula of Cornwall, and mainland Britain – boasts what must be one of the most spectacular, beautiful and exciting stretches of coastline in the world. Granite cliffs rise above a thundering sea. The South West Coast Path becomes technically challenging, with sections that necessitate scrambling over rocks and bog-hopping while narrow trails edge sheer drops. I find myself unexpectedly brimming with joy at simply being here. Having reached this point by running through a whole night. And knowing that every step brings me closer to the conclusion of this project.

I've rock climbed on the Cornish sea cliffs many times in the past and know how it feels to be a tiny dot amid the great, grey-gold expanses of those walls. We pass Bosigran – one of Cornwall's most famous rock-climbing areas – and I remember scrambling the famous Bosigran Ridge, also known as Commando Ridge, with Sim before we had the kids. Reaching the start of the climb requires a descent on uncertain holds, with safe but big backward moves above a yawning void of air and sea. I remember feeling delicate. Tired. Hormonal. I cried all the way down and laughed all the way back up again.

Today, Dave's brilliant, enthusiastic crew – Mike and Rachel – is waiting for us here. I made the decision not to have a crew because I wanted to see this race through under my own steam, but I hugely appreciate their cheerful presence as they pop up every few miles along the remainder of the route.

After headland followed by headland, steep, rocky, muddy ascent followed by steep, muddy, rocky descent, there's a glorious moment on the coast path when you crest the final hill above Clodgy Point and suddenly the whole of St Ives – framed by the white sand beaches at Porthmeor and Porthminster – opens up below. After so long in the wilderness, having not run through any towns since Penzance, nearly 64 kilometres (40 miles) earlier, it's a strange but welcome feeling.

At 126 kilometres (78 miles), St Ives is the final checkpoint on the Arc route. I spot Kirsty outside, chatting with her crew and getting ready to leave. It's good to see her again, especially now I'm feeling so much better than when I last saw her at Penzance.

'See you at the finish!' we call to each other.

Arc Angels usher us into the Island Centre, where I eat the first proper food I've had this race – veggie chilli and rice. Right then, it's one of the best meals I've ever eaten. I drink two cups of coffee and tend to my feet, then spot Leah Atherton – better known as Poet on the Run – a friend and someone whose work, running and general approach to life I've admired for a long time. She's volunteering as one of the Angels, something she does every year. I'd spotted her briefly at the start as I was being carried past by a wave of overexcited runners, but now it's great to be able to catch up.

'Is there anything I can get you?' she asks as I get my kit together ready to leave.

There is, actually. On my way in, I'd spotted some slices of cake on a table and they had called to me in a way not much else had for what feels like days. Leah packages some up in a sandwich bag that I stuff into a pocket in my pack. Together, the cake and Leah's belief and encouragement will keep me going over the final 40 kilometres (25 miles).

The St Ives checkpoint is known for its tight cutoff, which follows the night run and long, difficult section around Pendeen. Many runners will be timed out here, withdrawn from the race and ferried to the finish. It's something Dave and I have been worried about since setting out on our long walk from Land's End. But I remember race director Andrew

THE PATH WE RUN

'Ferg' Ferguson saying that once you'd made it to St Ives you could walk to the finish with plenty of time. It's a huge relief to have made it.

I spot Dave, ready and waiting, and we head out together, power hiking through St Ives and up the long hill to Carbis Bay. Reaching the Hayle Estuary a little later, we can see Hayle Towans – the start of the section affectionately known by Arc runners as the Dunes of Doom – just across the water, a distance of perhaps 200 metres (656 feet). But our route takes us all the way around the estuarine mud flats, 4 kilometres (2.5 miles) or so of uninspiring, flat running, including a stretch of the busy B3301.

When we eventually reach the dunes, there's not much in the way of doom. It's a bright day with big seas and surfers dot the waves. I walked this section with the kids just a couple of days ago so I know where I'm going, weaving in and out of some of the dunes and following the undulating path over others. As we leave the dunes behind I start to feel tired. Having started the race at midday yesterday and run through the afternoon, the night and nearly a whole day, real fatigue kicks in for the first time as the light starts to fade again. Dave seems to be striding away from me and I tell him to go for it if he's feeling good.

'We're finishing this together,' he says. 'You're the reason I carried on, so I'm not finishing it without you.'

I appreciate it. And I appreciate the cup of tea his crew hands me at Godrevy, where Dave sees hundreds of seals but I can't see any at all. This is the first indication that perception and reality are slipping apart. To this day I still don't know if there were any seals . . .

From St Ives to Godrevy, the route is relatively flat and thoroughly runnable had we been in a state to run at all. But not having managed a practice run of the last stretch, I'm blissfully unaware of the sting in the tail of this race, which awaits us between here and the finish at Porthtowan. I've heard about the infamous climb up to the finish at the Eco Park – just under a mile of steeply winding footpath – but no one has prepared me for the ordeal we must endure first. On this stretch of the coast path, two long and super-steep stepped climbs and descents tick off Porth-Cadjack Cove and Carvannel Downs. The runners have until this point been relatively spread out but are now bunched together as they crawl up these vicious ascents and crab-walk back down again. Out of context, in daylight, this would have been an incredibly bizarre sight to behold.

We run through Portreath, its streets dark and empty save for a few crews awaiting their runners. Dave happily chews his way through a sausage roll and a doughnut, but I'm struggling again and can't face food. It's frustrating, especially as the regular buffets are usually one of my favourite things about ultramarathons.

Further on, as dusk turns to dark once more, we're following a track along the perimeter fence of RRH Portreath at Nancekuke, a former chemical-weapons facility. As if it were the most normal thing in the world, I spot Kep waiting patiently at the side of the trail, paws crossed, eyes fixed on mine in the light of my headtorch. As I get closer, though, he melts away, leaving only a bush. Then I spot the huge Nancekuke radar dome, topped with a red light, a well-known local landmark. Only it's not behaving as it should be. It's following us. Every time I look to my right, the dome is there, keeping pace with us. It makes the hairs on the back of my neck prickle.

'Dave!' I shout. Dave is a few paces ahead, torch focused on the ground in front of his feet. I look to my right again. Sure enough, the ball is gliding along silently next to us, a dark bulk against a slightly lighter sky, red light glowing ominously.

'Dave . . . Is that thing following us?'

In the moment, this feels like a perfectly sensible question, but in the pause that follows, waiting for an answer, I feel a hint of embarrassment. Maybe I was mistaken. But I check again and there's the dome, still there, and still clearly moving.

'No idea,' comes the reply. 'I can't look or I'll fall over.'

Running past RRH Portreath that night, I have no idea of its history. I'll later discover that the last batch of Sarin nerve agent was manufactured here in 1977 and the facility demolished and buried in 1980. In my suggestible state, perhaps I picked up on something in the feel of the place.

There are two more precipitously steep lots of steps to negotiate, the first at Hayle Ulla and the second at Sally's Bottom – a place Dave's been looking forward to reaching all day. It starts to rain and I pull up my hood and switch on a podcast to distract myself from the interminable steps, the darkness, the rain and the worry that someone at the top might topple backwards and take us all out like dominoes on their way down.

At long, long last, we make the final descent into the village of Porthtowan. It's shortly after 8pm and Angels in high-vis jackets wait for us, pointing the way along lanes shiny with rain. After all this time, I can hardly believe it's nearly over. There are perhaps 15 minutes left until I cross the line. Sim and the kids will be there already – I can feel their nearness.

We turn off the lane onto the zigzag path up the last climb. I look up, a snake of glowsticks lighting the way. Lots of people, including most recently Mel, have warned me about this hill – another blow after more than 100 miles. But following the hell of the steps, and with the sounds of the finish line tantalizingly close, it's nowhere near as bad as I'm expecting.

Following the trail, following Dave's feet upwards, picking out the lights as we go, I try to tune into my sleep-deprived brain for these final moments. Now that I know beyond any doubt that I'm going to finish – not just this 100-mile race, the Arc of Attrition, the toughest winter 100-miler in the UK, but also my long fought-for dream of completing 100 miles – I want to savour it.

Dave and I fist-bump as we reach the top.

'We did it,' he says.

'We did!'

The narrow path opens onto grass and we run side-by side, following a string of lights around the final corner and onto the finishing strait. And just like that, there's the end. Time seems to slow as we approach the finish line, stretching out into the last few metres of effort, the longed-for moment when we can simply stop inching closer, and then hits hyper-speed as we cross it.

We step into something that's altogether different from the world we've inhabited for the past 32 hours and 40 minutes. People, cheering, photos, congratulations. I spot Sim and the kids and hug them tight. Dave gets a hug, too. It feels overwhelmingly good to stop and I'm not sure I can take another step. But then the next runners are coming in – it's time for them to have their moment – and we're channelled out of the cool, damp darkness of the January night and into the busy and brightly lit interior of the Eco Centre. It's all too much to process – the sudden return to light and sound and people. Race director Jane presents me with my 100-mile buckle and I clutch it in my hands, deliriously happy and trying to decide if I'm going to pass out, be sick, or both. We have our photos taken – I'm mostly grateful for a chair to sit down on.

Back outside, I find Sim and the kids and we make our way through the dark car park to where Kep – the real Kep – is waiting to wash the salt from my hands. Sitting in the car, experiencing stillness for the first time in nearly two days, I allow the mixture of emotions to flood through me: exhilaration, delight, joy. And relief. Relief that it is, at last, all over. And then all that's left is a strong desire to go home. It's as if I've spent all the energy it would take to be emotional on getting myself around 100 miles of the South West Coast Path and now have simply nothing left.

* * *

We drive along the dark emptiness of Cornish roads. Having had no more hallucinations since being chased by the military radar dome, I now find they blossom at every turn. I see a gorilla with glowing green eyes that melts into a bench and a bin as we draw alongside; an elderly woman with a sausage dog on a lead that becomes a street sign; herds of scurrying mice that make me think we're about to run them over until I realize they're just leaves.

It's delicious to simply sit, cradled in a down jacket; the soft warmth of the car seat beneath me, the dog on my feet and my family within touching distance. Even though I'm too wrecked to feel much, there's a noticeable sense of a heavy weight having been lifted. The question I've been asking of myself for the past year and a half now has an answer. Yes, I am capable of covering 100 miles on foot in one go. I even have a shiny silver buckle to prove it.

Back at the cottage, I hobble through the door, strip my muddy, sweaty kit off and get straight into the shower. I look at my body, somehow expecting to see something different from the last time I was there, yesterday morning. But it looks just the same, startlingly so. It's the same body. It's my body. And it was strong enough. And then sleep overtakes me – a great, sleepy wave so powerful it almost feels like nausea, except I'm not going to be sick; I'm going to fall asleep in the shower and I can't do that. I force myself out into the cold air, shivering violently, barely able to pull on a few clothes before bed and sleep swallow me whole. Sim brings a cup of tea in a few minutes later, but I don't find it until the following morning. Then, parched and grateful, I down it cold.

14

AFTERMATH

'The aftermath – the week after the Spine – I think it
was worse than the race itself. It was like someone had
taken out my soul – emptied me – I just had nothing.'
—Eddie Sutton, Winter Spine Race and
Northern Traverse podium finisher

The days after the Arc are a necessary sequence of
packing, cleaning, driving, unpacking and settling back
into our normal routines. A week passes. Emotions that
start with a brief peak of euphoria, followed by relief at having
at long last achieved my 100-mile goal, slump into a dull
sense of just being a little bit broken. It's hard to describe the
place I find myself in once the initial sense of achievement has
passed. I wallow, slow in thought and movement. Schedules,
appointments and deadlines slip through my fingers like
sand. I feel like I'm coming down with something, but
that something never materializes; so I hang here, between
sickness and health, wondering what I've done.

My body hasn't felt like this before. My feet hurt, which

is to be expected. The soles are still puffy and tender and the heels a little raw. More alarming, though, is my heavy breathing and pounding heart after even minor exertions like walking upstairs. I'm also, oddly, not hungry. Usually after an ultra I'll have a few days of feeling ravenous, scavenging from the fridge and cupboards whenever I get the chance. It's something I look forward to, that makes me feral and alive. But this time I wait and never feel hungry. I feel, instead, as if I'm fading, listless, grey.

There's also the sense of something amazing being over. Something I've worked on and thought about for so many months that's now simply over. As Hugo says, as we talk about it one evening: 'I thought finishing your 100-mile race would be a really big thing. But you just did it, and now it's . . . done.'

Before, when I'd failed to finish, or even failed to start, there had been jeopardy; emotions had run high, and there was another race to train for and plan for. But now, suddenly, after so many months of training and planning and uncertainty, I've answered the question of my capabilities. Here, in the aftermath, I don't feel the need to discover any further limits. I've no more races planned. I feel empty, spent. And a bit crap.

I've often heard people talk about post-adventure blues. I've always assumed it was just a comedown after so much planning and preparation and the excitement of getting the challenge done. But what are we really chasing when we set ourselves big goals? And what are we really getting out of them? If we're not happy with our lives outside our adventures, the adventures won't solve anything; they'll just press pause for a bit longer. And if we are happy, then what price are we paying when we spend vast sums of time, money and . . . what feels like health credits . . . on the pursuit? At some of my darkest moments, I rage against the privilege of it all – I think that perhaps ultrarunning is a pastime for those with too much time, too much money and too much comfort. Those for whom being broken for weeks afterwards isn't too much of a problem.

In her book on transformative experiences, professor of philosophy and cognitive science Laurie Ann Paul suggests that we can choose to have experiences because of what these experiences reveal to us, rather than because they are intrinsically enjoyable. These experiences might involve sustained effort, or even sustained suffering. It's not all finish line photos and happily ever after, but it's in this effort and suffering that we grow.

In everyday life, we spend a lot of time avoiding unpleasant experiences and seeking out pleasant ones. But when we choose to subject ourselves to an experience that we know will be difficult, painful, lengthy and challenging – one that will cause us, in some way, to suffer – we can accept this for what the experience reveals to and about us.

I'd set out on my quest to run 100 miles precisely to have one of these revelatory experiences. I thought that completing a 100-mile race would reveal something about myself – that I was tougher, stronger, more resilient and braver than I feared I might be – and something about others; what it was that all those ultrarunners I so admired were experiencing. Now, on the other side of that challenge, I've certainly had revelations – but they aren't the ones I was expecting.

Perhaps one of the reasons there are fewer women on the start lines of ultras, and especially longer ultras, is that they don't feel as much need to seek experiences that reveal hidden depths of strength, resilience and awesomeness. Perhaps life as a woman, navigating regular bodily discomforts and threats to our safety while embodying the resilience and patience required for caring, demands enough of us already, revealing these facets of our characters to us over and over again. By contrast, are men who experience insufficient stimulus in their working lives craving the physical suffering they've evolved to withstand – seeking out hardship that reveals the strength and resilience of their character in ultrarunning and other extreme challenges?

Maybe for these reasons it's the case that women who run ultras simply run fewer of them. I've tried and so far failed to find data on the frequency with which women and men participate in ultras. Are the start-line statistics skewed by the men who run an ultra every month and the women who run one or two a year? It's something I'll continue trying to discover.

Emma ran the Arc of Attrition in 2023, finishing first woman, fourth overall and setting a new women's record in the process. I tell her my time was 11 hours slower than hers, but Emma's quick to deflect this, telling me she's in awe of those who are out there pushing the cut-offs, finishing 100-mile races 10, even 20 hours behind the winners.

'In many ways it's so much harder,' she says. 'Because they're just out there for so long, often with no sleep. At Tor des Geants (a 330-kilometre non-stop ultramarathon in Italy's Aosta Valley, which Emma won in 2023) I finished on the Wednesday – there were still people coming in on the Friday and Saturday. It's crazy to be out for that length of time.'

Emma's first 100-mile race followed the Lady Anne's Way, linking up Skipton and Penrith via a series of ruined castles built by the formidable 17th-century landowner, Lade Anne Clifford. 'I'm big into history, so it was a perfect race for me. It's beautiful, quite runnable, and finishes on my local trails – I had to run past my house in the last couple of miles, which was hard! But I loved it and realised that was the distance for me.' Emma finished first woman and second overall in under 20 hours, an incredible result for a first 100-miler from another formidable woman.

I loved racing in the Arc of Attrition. I loved the buzz, the camaraderie, the support, the kindness and the community. I discovered those inner reserves of strength that I'd hoped I had all along. But, almost more than the race itself, it was the training that delivered revelations by the bucketload. Getting to the top of the Grand Mont, the highest I'd ever been on foot, was a truly revelatory and transformative experience. Making my way up, meeting no other human being on the way, scrambling the lunar landscape with no tracker, no support crew, no race safety team, just me and my moment-by-moment decisions that would determine the outcome. With an eye on the incoming weather front, I'd pushed on through real, relevant fear, judging – correctly, as it turned out – that I had just enough time to summit and get back down before the weather broke. I felt utterly vital, utterly alive and, for quite a bit of the time, utterly terrified. But the sense of achievement, and the knowledge that I was physically and mentally stronger that I'd thought, fundamentally changed something I knew about myself. It was the same when I scrambled the Nantlle Ridge in Snowdonia, when I ran long sections of the Beacons Way in South Wales and even when I tackled the infamous stretch of the South West Coast Path between Cape Cornwall and St Ives on that ice-cold morning with the dog. These were the moments that had simultaneously revealed and forged new strengths.

Back in my post-100-mile funk, I discover that there may be a reason I'm not bouncing back as quickly as I'd hoped. A routine blood test picks up that my ferritin level is very low – in other words, that I have an iron deficiency. I'm told to book an appointment with a doctor. It's all a bit of a shock. I take care with my diet and, although I'm vegetarian, I think I eat lots of food containing iron. Mostly, it's an odd feeling knowing that there's something 'wrong' with me that I didn't know about before and that I'm still unsure about the seriousness of it. I send Renee a message with my numbers to see if it's really a problem – if there's anyone who knows about these things it's Renee – but she's far from reassuring.

'I'm surprised you can walk, let alone run,' she replies.

I book the appointment and spend the next few days researching low ferritin levels in runners. It's surprisingly common, especially in women – around 50 per cent of female endurance athletes suffer from some degree of iron deficiency. It probably explains a lot – my low mood since the race, the lack of hunger, the heart palpitations and breathlessness. The doctor gives me iron tablets and within a week I'm feeling better in every way.

I set out on this project hoping to find that, as a woman in my 40s who's always been reasonable at sport but certainly nowhere near elite, ultrarunning might offer me a space where I could still flourish. A place where I didn't feel past it – on a gradual but inevitable decline that would see me, along with my hair, gradually fade into greyness. I had wondered whether this might be a place where I could tackle the popular debate about whether women can beat men over longer distances. Whether we have secret powers of endurance that emerge only when all the men have powered themselves into oblivion. But, in the end, I discovered something much more important: that this sport is about people, about humanity.

As Courtney Dauwalter put it when I asked her whether she thought women would ever routinely beat men over ultra distances: because so many factors other than physical prowess come into play as the distances get longer and the challenges stack up, it's not really about sex or gender or muscles or VO$_2$max. Ultrarunning gives each individual human the opportunity to train hard, think hard and prepare hard – and then to utilize their own unique skill set to progress over the required distance as well as they can. The range of possible ultrarunning challenges, from a fastest known time (FKT) on a local long-distance trail to the biggest 100-mile races in the world, means that everyone can take on a challenge that is best suited to their specific set of skills and preferences. Whether you're someone who finds joy in the simplicity of spending 24 hours running round a track, someone who longs for the remote ruggedness of the mountains, or someone who likes to mix it up and try a bit of everything, there's an ultramarathon for you. For the vast majority of participants, prizes, podiums and PBs become utterly meaningless as the bigger story of the race unfolds. Instead, the rewards lie in discovering who we are, who we want to be and how we cope with the space that lies between.

Running 100 miles is both huge and, in the grander scheme of things, tiny. In some ways, it's important: the human stories, the shared experiences and forged bonds, the self-discovery, the stepping outside of everyday life to learn new things about our bodies and minds. But in others it's insignificant and even unwise. Voluntary suffering is, after all, a privilege that many people aren't afforded. Spending so much of my time over the past year and more obsessed with and immersed in the world of ultrarunning, I've thought long and hard about these questions. Training for ultramarathons gives you plenty of time to think.

During the process of running 100 miles, I've learned things about myself that, without some pretty serious life events, I'd never otherwise have had the opportunity to discover. And that's a great thing. When I consider how I felt on the Beacons Way Ultra 100 that I didn't finish and the Arc, which I did, I realize I felt far better on the former. And yet I gave up, thinking at the time that that was my only option. Now I know, without any doubt, that I could have carried on. I know I could have finished. The obstacle that felt so insurmountable existed only in my head.

Looking back on the path I've run, not only while working towards this specific goal but also with a wider lens on life and running in general, I realize that my decision to sometimes step away when things hurt isn't representative of my failings – although this has certainly been how I've seen it on occasion. It's because I've become kinder to myself, more respectful of my body and the limits of my resources. Whereas in my 20s I demanded of myself, punished myself, judged, lectured and reprimanded myself, I now must ask nicely. Having been broken and repaired in so many ways on so many occasions, my body no longer simply responds to my whim. It needs nurturing, maintaining, understanding. I can still do hard things, but I need to do them in mutual agreement with my body.

Completing 100 miles depended on the physical body

I was able to line up at the start with. How well I'd looked after it in the lead up to the race: my diet and sleep, my training and rest, the attention I'd paid to the voice of my physical body. It also depended upon my emotional self: my relationships with those around me, my mood, focus, resilience and willingness to push myself beyond comfort and rationality. It was the union of all these things that forged a new kind of strength.

I'd also connected with so many people in the ultrarunning community. The sense of belonging I'd longed for but felt was missing when I returned to endurance sport as a mother had been thoroughly restored. Now, I felt at home in this body that had given me so much in so many different ways. I felt connected with all the runners I'd run with, chatted with and interviewed, and whose stories I'd followed with awe and fascination. I also felt part of the bigger story of women's sport throughout history, which has at times been clear and easy to follow and at others fragmented, or even lost altogether. I thought of the pedestriennes who'd broken rules and records in the late 1800s and the ultrarunners doing the same a century later. The surge in women's ultra-distance sport that we're seeing today has happened before; but this time we must make sure we build on it, generation after generation, so our daughters and granddaughters and great-granddaughters never have to start from the beginning again.

EPILOGUE

Two months after finishing the Arc of Attrition, I suddenly realize that running feels good again. I have that sense of possibility back in my legs and a question gradually making itself heard in my mind: what next?

I've explored what it was like to run in the mountains – so many different mountains on different days in different conditions – but I still haven't run 100 mountainous miles, which was my original goal. There are other ways to run the distance, too – on the track, for instance, like many of ultrarunning's greatest female protagonists have done. There are backyard ultras, the mental game of which I find intriguing, and self-devised ultradistance challenges that test all your amassed learning to complete solo, with no aid stations or route markers to help. After my disappointing DNF at the Beacons Way Ultra, I'll be returning to have another go, bringing in all the lessons I've learned since. I also have a yearning to go back and run the Arc again, but better, in full knowledge that it's something I can do.

Immediately after the Arc, I couldn't put my finger on exactly how running 100 miles had changed me, but the perspective I've gained over the past few weeks has made several things clearer. I'm no longer afraid of running through the night – in fact, running through a whole night, seeing the sun set, the light of the full moon on the sea and then the sun rise again was an incredible experience that I now treasure. I also have a new sense of being capable of achieving more than I believed I could. Belief is important, but we shouldn't be limited by our beliefs. What if they sell us short?

I think of Courtney Dauwalter's pain cave and wonder whether I really, fully visited it. Had I been too hesitant, too afraid, to really get deep into my own cave and discover where my limits lay or had I loitered at the entrance? In my avoidance of risk and pushing too hard to get that 100-mile finish, had I allowed self-preservation to stop me from truly experiencing the transcendent moments many ultrarunners describe? The pain cave is calling. I feel a rising curiosity now, a yearning, even, to pay it another visit soon.

With the resurgence in ultrarunning over the past decade, women across the world are clearly rediscovering what it means to run a long way. During Women's History Month in March 2024, 42-year-old Camille Herron of the US broke the women's 6-day record, running 901 kilometres (560 miles) around a track during Lululemon's FURTHER event, which brought together 10 women who had never competed at this distance before. Camille averaged 150 kilometres (93 miles) of running a day and broke a total of

11 world records in the process. The event was also utilized as a research study, with sport scientists collecting data from the runners to further our knowledge of the female body in ultrarunning. Prior to FURTHER, New Zealand runner Sandra Barwick's six-day record of 883.6 kilometres (549 miles) had stood since 1990. Before that, Eleanor Robinson broke the record an incredible 6 times, raising the distance from 658 kilometres (409 miles) in 1983 to 866 kilometres (538 miles) in 1989. Shortly after Camille's astonishing performance came Jasmin Paris's Barkley Marathons finish followed in April by two more incredible performances by women: doctor and researcher Hannah Rickman finished first woman and second overall in the 300-kilometre Northern Traverse, despite a named storm blowing through mid-race. And Sarah Perry set a new self-supported FKT on the South West Coast Path, covering the 635 miles, alone and in tough conditions, in 13 days 11 hours 31 minutes and 20 seconds, beating both the existing women's and men's self-supported records. Every week, it seems, women are achieving greater things in the sport of ultrarunning. I hope we can keep this momentum going, following in the footsteps of those who ran before us and making things even better for those to come.

Jasmin finished the Barkley Marathons against – but also because of – so many odds. In many ways, her upbringing and subsequent adventures set the scene for her achievements. But that doesn't take away from the graft she must have put in, alongside being a mum and a vet. I think about all those mornings before work when she ran, through the dark, the rain, the discomforts of winter. The night she got up at midnight and spent nine hours running up and down a local mountain, the rain turning to snow each time she climbed higher, and back to rain again on the way down. Every day since failing to finish Barkley the year before, fuelled by this fire, knowing how much more it would take, building a body and mind ready to take on that beast of a course and triumph. I can't help, as I fight my way through weather and mud and hills and fatigue of the wettest spring in living memory, channelling Jasmin just a little. 'I did it for women,' she said when the BBC interviewed her a couple of days after her finish. And I can feel her strength and courage and determination flowing through me, too.

Jasmin's achievement really does matter – in both the doing and the telling. This message of persisting and enduring, of strength, determination and self-belief really does reach out and touch all women, all runners, everyone who hears it. I've watched the footage of her finish, seen the utter determination turn in an instant to utter exhaustion the moment she reaches the yellow gate. I know it so well now I can play it on a loop in my mind. It's captured something that's been shared hundreds of thousands of times. Jasmin is extraordinary; and yet she's ordinary, too. She's an example of what you can do – what *we* can do, if we want it enough, believe it enough, and if we're given the education and support we need to realize our dreams. If Jasmin can do it – if she can put in the work, tolerate the discomfort, make the time – then so can I. I won't ever achieve her levels of greatness in running, but I can put as much effort and commitment in. In the aftermath of Barkley, I hear other women vocalizing these same feelings, too.

What Jasmin did was an incredibly powerful display of individual passion, dedication and endeavour; but it was so much more than that. So few men can finish Barkley. Relative to those who've stood at the start line, it's a tiny percentage. But given how few women even start the race, the likelihood of one of them finishing is miniscule. Miniscule and yet possible. And Jasmin, after two previous attempts, was convinced it was possible for her. Barkley is so much more about the 'other' factors – those elements beyond muscular strength and maximal aerobic capacity. To succeed here demands outstanding skills in navigation, problem-solving, self-management, fatigue resistance, sleep-deprivation endurance and a willingness to just keep going when almost everyone else would quit. These are all basic survival skills that our ancestors would have known and possessed to simply stay alive, but that have been lost to most and continue to vanish as technology lulls us into false trust. They remain important, though, and they can and should be taught from an early age. Humanity's path is leading into a new unknown; and the skills gained by learning how to survive, problem-solve, be resourceful and take care of ourselves and others may be the ones that save us. Ultrarunning gives us the opportunity to test out our skills, to see how we'd manage in a crisis, to learn how much further we can go, long after our bodies and brains are telling us to stop.

I'm also inspired everyday by the stories of those who aren't making headlines but take on big challenges purely for the personal sense of achievement. The women who are discovering ultrarunning for the first time in their 30s, 40s, 50s and beyond. The women who are realizing that it's not just something they're capable of doing, but that they actually have a wealth of skills and abilities that lend themselves perfectly to enduring over long distances in a range of environments. I want to hear those women talking about how they've surprised themselves; how they'd never thought of ultramarathons as something they could do; how everyone thought they were mad but they went out and did it anyway. These stories fill me with joy every time I hear them.

Ultrarunning is unique because we all line up on the same start line – elites, midpackers and backmarkers together. And once we cross that start line, giving ourselves over to the adventure, the uncertainty, the pain and the joy that is to come, the path we run is one forged by those who ran before us, one shared with those who run beside us, and one we're blazing for those to come.

ACKNOWLEDGEMENTS

A huge thank you to all the incredible ultrarunning women who generously shared their time, wisdom and 100-mile stories with me during the running and writing of this book, including Jasmin Paris, Courtney Dauwalter, Lucy Bartholomew, Emma Stuart, Chrissie Wellington, Eleanor Robinson, Beth Pascall, Diana Fitzpatrick, Kirsty Reade, Renee McGregor, Sabrina Verjee, Sabrina Pace-Humphreys, Holly Stables, Debbie Martin-Consani, Anna Troup, Milly Troup, Amy Fulford, Sophie Power, Eddie Sutton, Allie Bailey, Melissa Nicholas, Sam Hudson Figueira and Katie Holmes.

To Dave 'Red Shorts Guy' Vickerstaff and his crew, Mike and Rachel; to everyone else I've shared miles with on the trails over the years, or who has helped me to keep going with cake and kind words – you are too numerous to list but include: The Arc Angels, Leah Atherton, Amy Freeman, Claire Bishop, Hannah Large, Hannah Bown, Hugh Marsden, Fred Fox, Ros Shuttleworth; Elle Wood at Limitless Trails; Mudcrew Jane Stephens and Andrew

Ferguson; Mark Brooks at Outer Edge Events; David Miller for the beautiful cover shot, and continuing to do such important work capturing images of great ultrarunning stories; the world's best running buddies Emma and Anita, and their families; Zoe and Jen; Damian Hall; Bethan Taylor-Swaine; Dr Carla Meijen; Dr Nick Tiller; Dr Emma Cowley; Dr Sarah Bosch; Clive Allen/La Sportiva; Nicola Frow/Beta Running/Ultimate Direction/Kahtoola; Leki UK; Georgie Tweddle; Penny and Nick at Threshold Sports; Michael Jones; Marie Cheng; Hayden Arrowsmith; and Steve and Kate at Lana's Lodge.

And to Trevor Davies, Rimsha Falak and the team at Octopus Publishing Group; my agent, Kirsty McLachlan; my wolf in spaniel's clothing Kep; Lucy and Sam and family; the Perkins and Benson families; and to the loves of my life, Eva, Hugo and Sim.

INDEX